D0491059

ORIGINAL JOY
free the playful child in you

ORIGINAL JOY
free the playful child in you

Joseph G. Donders & Elizabeth Byrne

TWENTY-THIRD PUBLICATIONS
Mystic, Connecticut

Twenty-Third Publications
185 Willow Street
P.O. Box 180
Mystic, CT 06355
(203) 536-2611

© 1989 by Joseph Donders and Elizabeth Byrne.
All rights reserved. No part of this publication
may be reproduced in any manner without prior
written permission of the publisher. Write to Per-
missions Editor.

ISBN: 0-89622-388-4
Library of Congress Card Catalog Number 88-51809

Other Books by Joseph Donders

Creation and Human Dynamism

Empowering Hope:
Thoughts to Brighten Your Day

The Global Believer:
Toward a New Imitation of Christ

CONTENTS

ORIGINAL JOY
free the playful child in you

INTRODUCTION

*Anyone who does not welcome the Kingdom of God
as a little child shall not enter it.*

Jesus

There is something touching about a child,
there is something touching about each child,
especially when the child is small.
Children often seem so serenely complete,
so one with the breast,
still near the womb
when they were one with it all.
    You can see it in the way they play,
    without fear, freely relating,
    you can see it in the way
    they look around themselves
    in their wide open world.
The break up and disintegration
of our lost Self in adult life,
remains the paradigm and criterion
of all our desires.
    It is from that hidden and repressed source
    that human cultures generated
    their visions of paradise,
    of a world with the whole of creation at play,
    a world in unity
    beyond death, hunger, and shortage.
The serene completeness

of our early childhood
lodged in our heart and memory
remains as a dream.
It haunts us
in our moments of depression.[1]
   In thousands and millions of ways,
   we were born
   from connections with nature,
   from uniting and loving bonds,
   from moments of ecstasy into a world alone.
That lonesomeness only slowly dawns upon us,
the young child does not experience it as yet,
reaching out for the sky
with its little hands,
stamping space open with its tiny feet
looking for light, color, and form
with wide open eyes,
listening to sounds, music
and the murmur of endless words,
smelling and tasting nipple and milk
salty, sweet, wet, and fragrant,
being touched softly and lovingly,
smiled at,
and the center of the whole wide world.
   A delight that can rudely be broken,
   but never completely lost.
   Sometimes it finds
   a glimpse of expression
   when we are united in love,
   or when beauty comforts us.
An ideal that remains hidden deep in us,
even if education, socialization, regimentation,
legalized religion, inflicted conformism,
disappointments and betrayals
disconnected us
from that wealth deep in ourselves,
breaking the bonds
that even then keep us alive.
   It is only when growing up,
   that we can reconnect,
   reaching deep in ourselves,

rebonding,
finding the ourselves we lost,
hearing, seeing, smelling, feeling,
touching again
the delight of life.
Not everyone does, not everyone knows,
women mostly quicker than men.
Not everyone remembers.
Some never lost their childhood vision,
they remained sincerely devoted to self
all their life,
They lived the fullest possible life,
even conquered death,
and set us an example:
Jesus, Martin Luther King, Gandhi,
Buddha, Michelangelo, Einstein,
and so many other mystics, artists, and saints.
This book will help you
to remember before you began to forget
the one you were,
and can be again:
life delighting in self.

CHAPTER ONE

SEEDS OF GLORY

The seed of God is in us.
Now the seed of a pear tree grows into a pear tree
and a hazel seed into a hazel tree;
a seed of God grows into God.

Meister Eckhart

Do you remember when you were first a child.
Nothing in the world seemed strange to you?
You perceived, for the first time, shapes already familiar,
And seeing, you knew that you have always known
The lichen on the rock, fern-leaves, the flowers of
*   thyme,*
As if the elements newly met in your body,
Caught up into the momentary vortex of your living
Still kept the knowledge of a former state,
In you retained recollection of clouds and oceans,
The branching tree, the dancing flame.

Kathleen Raine

On either side of the river were the trees of life.
The leaves of the tree were for the healing of the nations.

Book of Revelation 22:2

The sun is shining,
birds are chirping through your window.
It is quiet. You switch on the radio. You read a book.
You listen to someone.
Listening and being moved by someone else,
by more than one, by many.
> You and I, so locked up in ourselves,
> so individualized,
> so certain of the uniqueness of our experience,
> our time and place in the mystery of life,
> are in contact with all those others,
> relating to them, speaking, dancing, singing,
> touching, smelling, loving, and sometimes hating.
Locked up and yet open, isolated but not insulated,
devoted to myself and yet tied to all those others
by affection and my faith in them.
And so it can go on
—when we are at our best and not depressed—
the whole day,
with all of us,
talking, laughing, looking serious,
reacting to what we saw or heard,
having our thoughts and feelings,
being our uniqueness
together with all those others
as full of themselves and the universe,
as you and we are full of ourselves and the universe.
Are you never struck
by the mystery you are?
There is something mysterious about us.
There is something mysterious about me.
There is something mysterious about you.
It is not mysterious really.
It is the way we are.
Carriers of an inner secret.
Mysteries. Paradoxes. Doubles.
One unique point in time and space,
and yet at the same time all time and space.
One individual
—undivided in ourselves and divided from all the others—
and yet the whole of creation.

One bundle of experiences, one stream of consciousness,
yet open to all experience, to all consciousness.
An inner filled with reminiscences
hidden away,
until—now and then—
they suddenly pop up and come out.
    Are we really the individuals
    we are supposed to be in this modern world,
    in this new world society?
    Aren't we all
    connected in so many ways
    with the world around us?
Make the test for yourself.
Take an empty sheet of paper.
Write a word in the center of it.
Any word you can think of will do.
Draw a circle around that word
and take some time to write down
the persons, the things, the events
that word makes you think of.
Indicate those associations
in one or two words only.
You will be amazed
at the clusters that form themselves,
at the patterns you will discover.
You are tapping the richness of yourself,
your history and your memories.
And, yes, you could have taken any word at all.
Every single word can serve as an entry,
a key to yourself.
We are interconnected, attracting and attracted.
We realize it when we say:
"We live in a small world,"
every time we meet an unexpected friend in a far-off place,
a relation or a connection
we never thought of before.
It is only when attracted by the universe
that you find your real name and full calling.

    You were called by a name,
    from the very beginning

by those who represented life and Mother Earth
around you.
Your first name, the name,
that makes you a special person,
that separates you
and distinguishes you from other people,
but at the same time unites you
with those who call you.
Your name makes you a sharer in the world.
Every time it is called,
even in an ordinary conversation,
you feel some warmth,
it is as if you are plucked
like the string of a harp, piano or violin,
and not only you, but your world
—the whole universe—
starts to vibrate.
Do you remember the experience
of not being introduced to a group of people
you happen to be with?
It is a very unpleasant experience.
You don't seem to count. In fact you don't.
Being called holds the promise of relationship
in whose warmth you will unfold
as a flower unfolds to the sun.
Your mother, friends, and lover
call and say your name
in the most intimate, lovely, and promising way.
Your family name connects you
through parents to ancestors,
while together your names suggest
connection and uniqueness,
a creative tension which will last throughout life.

A single leaf of a tree is beautiful,
yet its life depends on vital life-juice which it receives
through its connection to the tree.
Likewise you and I on the Tree of Life.
Do you remember
when you were a child
and wide awake to the call of life within you?

Who ignited you
—every child is inflammable,
not one is fireproof—
We were exquisitely formed
in our mother's womb
of cherished protons
from the original creation of the universe.
We grew to the rhythm of her heartbeat
and to the sound of her voice.
At birth she filled our senses:
her breasts awakened
our smell, touch and taste,
her hands made our body tingle
with its first excitement all over,
while her face was our first focus.
Her warmth, protection and love
kindled the spark of life within us
and made the world around shine.
From all over the world Joseph Chilton Pearce collected
research material that speaks to this process.
He speaks of a "trigger-off" effect.
When a child is born, it is able to see,
touch, hear, smell, and taste.
Those possibilities or potentialities have to germinate.
They have to be ignited in the right way.
If things are left to nature
this sparking off works beautifully.
    The child starts to see
    seeing for the first time
    the triangle formed
    by the eyes and mouth of the mother,
    or any other face it sees first.
It starts to smell,
and will recognize the smell of the breast of its mother
for all feeding time to come,
once brought to its nipple.
    Every mother will immediately
    massage the newborn baby from top to toe
    energizing all nerve ends for the rest of life.
    The child begins to taste
    at the moment it feeds

for the first time.
Only hearing is already
triggered off in the womb,
and cells are formed,
vibrating to the sound of voices and music.
It is this natural process that is badly interrupted
when the child is born,
not into intimacy with mother and others,
but into the bluish glare of fluorescent light,
in a clinic with plastic, rubber, and metal,
surrounded by people who are wearing masks
and who manipulate all kinds of instruments and tools.
No wonder
that the child born in a hospital
smiles sometimes six months later
than the baby born of a mother
in the warmth of her home.

In case this first love fails not all hope is lost,
does a lover not ignite you in a similar way?
And what about some of your educators?
Do you remember your school days
and who influenced you most amongst your teachers?
Some seemed to ignite your inner spark
with a secret power that flowed into you.
Through their integrity and aliveness
they energized your growth
from the fullness of their being.
They initiated you into lifelong interests.
Others hardly did that.
They are not the ones we remember immediately,
when asked who influenced us most in life.
Those others influenced you.
They helped you to grow into the one you became
and are becoming.
A biology teacher appeared to see
the wonder of life in everything.
He almost lived it.
An art teacher dressed in a way that showed,
that she saw not only one shape,

but also all the shapes around it.
Another teacher shared chemical experiments,
while another tuned into your inner melody
and awoke a lifelong joy of music.
A religious teacher spoke in mystical terms
about the possibility we all have
to enter into our inner selves,
or about humanity forming together
with the whole of nature
a kind of body where all and everything
was (and is) pulsing together.
Others you remember
because of their friendliness and interest in you,
not only and not even primarily as a student,
but as a person.
  A glance through these memories
  reveals that teachers who influenced us most
  recognized no personal or interest boundaries
  but are the ones who understood that our name
  relates us to everything.
They lived their priorities
and were concerned with the roots
as well as with the branches of learning.
They remained connected with the vital life-juice.
They had no subject-object relationship
with their field of learning
but incarnated and manifested it in their being.
Their field was illuminated with a dimension
which was poetic and mystical, aesthetic and mythical,
which transcended the world of facts.
Physics was to do with the Dance of Creation
and geography with the radiance of the sunset.
  They did not fence us in
  within the borders of a specialization,
  their hobby, a program,
  a textbook or examination requirements.
  They did not restrict us.
  They liberated us, they made us breathe
  like a child of the universe.
  They made us see,
  they made us connect with the others,
  people in the past, plants and animals,

growth, dying off, and the perpetual survival
in egg and seed.
They did not only give the answers,
they awoke our wonder and radical amazement.
They made you feel great in the water,
under the sky, in a garden, a park or a forest.
They made you feel fine when you stood nude
in nature self.
They made you feel a center where all and everything
really meets and comes together.
They revealed to us our place on the Tree of Life.
Meister Eckhart
—a medieval mystic—
believed that at the birth of each of us
the exuberant universe gathers herself
in shouts of joy.
Quite a thought
suggesting the enormous potential of each of us
for cherishing and changing our earth.
Parents and teachers who influenced you
recognized this hope and mystery,
and growing life in you.
They are the ones who did not attempt
to mold, form, or train us,
but who had faith in the human life-process
in its uniqueness and connectedness
horizontally through the world
and vertically through time.
They shared their passion and enthusiasm
for knowledge and enhanced creation
through their reverence for life
and through our "initiation" into
that fullness of reality.
The best and dearest ones
are those who reconnected us
with the universe.

Isn't that the joy we experience when relaxing
with a friend, who, loving and appreciating us,
unlocks all kinds of hidden potentialities in us—
not only spiritually or mentally,
but also physically and bodily?

You made me into the one I am!
Without you I would never have known,
I would never have experienced myself!
You made what was hidden within me
grow and bloom.
In each book, in each film,
in each conversation, in each meeting
there is the possibility
of a new barrier broken, a new vista discovered,
a new perspective unfolded,
a new attraction and allurement felt,
and another wall broken down.

Developing your thought,
encouraging it to bud and sprout in association
—as we suggested above—
you will see clusters grow and grow,
patterns emerge,
switches will be felt,
and the miracle we are will blossom,
because indeed we find our place,
time and space on that great Tree
connecting and vitalizing it all.
Although nature, home, street, family, school,
and media messages
stream into our consciousness,
is it not true that human relationships
have exerted the most powerful influence on your life?
Nothing can substitute
for the impact of
one person on another.
Alone we are incomplete.
In true friendship we are unique and universal
at one and the same time.
In dialogue we seek ourselves,
each other, and our mutual growth.
In listening and responding
hope, faith, and trust in self
are enhanced.
We are interconnected
and intersubjective
in a participatory universe.

CHAPTER TWO

A CONSPIRACY OF CO-EXISTENCE

We are not like flowers in a bunch but the leaves and flowers of a great tree on which each appears at its time and place according to the demands of the All.
Pierre Teilhard de Chardin

It is the light continually falling from heaven which also gives a tree the energy to send powerful roots into the earth. The tree is really rooted in the sky. It is only what comes from heaven that can make a real impress on the earth.
Simone Weil

We and the cosmos are one. The cosmos is a vast living body of which we are still part. The sun is a great heart whose tremors run through our smallest veins. The moon is a great gleaming nerve-center from which we quiver for ever. Who knows the power that Saturn has over us, or Venus? But it is a vital power, rippling exquisitely through us all the time.
D. H. Lawrence

In this century,
in this New Age,
in which many are no longer at ease,
and complaints about the state of the world
fill the air,
and threats to our existence are sensed everywhere,
what lovers, poets, and mystics
had always intuited, felt, and known
was rediscovered.
    The stories differ;
        experiences are the same.
He tells how one night he woke up,
there was a strange noise in a room
somewhere in the house,
carefully he went to have a look.
It was his pregnant cat
that had been looking for a hiding place.
Finally he could place the noise;
it was in a shelf in an open cupboard.
The noise changed to something like a cry for help,
his cat was having difficulties giving birth.
He could not do very much,
but when he crouched down on his knees
he looked straight in the eyes of the cat,
with the kitchen light reflected
in her deep, deep eyes,
and he knew, he felt,
a bond that remained with him
for days and days.
        She was sitting on the beach,
        the ocean was blue,
        the surf surging,
        the air fresh and full of heady fragrance.
        It was early in the morning,
        the rising sun crept slowly
        from the water over the yellow beach,
        reaching her.
        She started to cast a shadow in its light,
        caught in the orange-yellow ever more shiny light,
        seabirds were shouting,
        some fishermen—far away—

hauled in their nets.
It was like a landscape with figures
dancing all around her,
the sun and the clouds,
the colors and smells,
the green and the blue,
the salt and the sweet,
whirling atoms in cosmic oceans
dancing together with her in endless arrays.

Centuries ago
mystics of all traditions
realized that creation is a dynamic reality in process.
 In our days
 nuclear physicists seeking the ultimate substance
 of the hard billiard-ball-like atom of our school days
 have encountered a *wave* and *particle*
 at the same place and time.
 It defies analysis: it is all a dance which,
 —for our convenience—
 we divide in different movements.
An "atom," ultimately a set of relationships,
reaches out to others, dancing around with them.
As everything is composed of these elementary particles
—corn and cabbage, tortoise and goldfish,
cow and sheep, dog and cat,
you and me—
everything is related since the initial big bang:

> *To see the world in a grain of sand*
> *And heaven in a wild flower*
> *Hold infinity in the palm of our hand*
> *And eternity in an hour.*[1]

Each of us is in, and of, the cosmic web.
Each is a focus, a point, a concrescence
where rays of life interconnect.
 Each is a unique and universal rhythmic pulse:
 particle and wave.
 Each human being born
 is a center of energy and potency

awaiting ignition.
One focus influences all others
with its light and its warmth.
If one focus of the web is shaken or damaged
all other parts of the web,
are shaken and damaged, too.
 In this way each of us is diminished
 by hurt to the other
 and each is augmented
 when another's anonymity turns to glory.
 Is that why we have
 the strange habit of bringing our hands together
 to applaud when one of us is successful?
The applause we give
to an orchestra and its conductor,
to researchers and their teams,
to a peacemaker after a happy outcome,
to an athlete after a brilliant performance,
is the applause we give to all of us,
ourselves included.
Their success is our achievement,
they do not only show what they can do,
but what we can do.
Their glory brightens our day.
As Christy Nolan,
the seriously disabled poet and author, said:
each acknowledgment of my talent
raises all disabled people
by revealing their inner power and possibilities.
Landing on the moon by some meant
that *we* landed on the moon.
 Much has recently been written in the West
 about the essential nature of a human being
 which remains a mystery.
 Are we born noble or evil,
 or neither good nor evil?
This question was asked
in the multi-cultural
and interreligious context of Kestrel Manor School
in Nairobi, Kenya, East Africa in the Eighties.
Parents and teachers experienced vague unease.

The answers given suggest
that African and Asian views
of human nature are more positive
than Western views.
The majority of parents and teachers
believed that a child was born
neither good nor evil.[2]
Of the other parents thirty-five percent,
including sixty-seven percent of African parents
and eighty-nine percent of Asian parents,
believed a child to be born noble,
while a small minority (all Western)
believed she was born evil.
That the African and Asian view
of the essential nature of a human being
is more positive than the Western view
is worthy of comment.

The writers of the psalms in the Old Testament
and Jesus in the New Testament
frequently reminded people
of their royal personhood and divine dignity.
These have been replaced in the Western tradition
with a fall/redemption theology of sin.
God has changed from Someone
who holds a child cheek to cheek
to a distant, unmoved, judgmental
and absolute masculine Father God.
Christianity has relatively recently come to East Africa
and traditional concepts remain.
God is the Mother, Father, and Parent,
the Comforter, who is close to people
and provides for them.
She is the Artist-in-Chief
and not immediately involved
in keeping the moral order.
In Asian Creation myths
the neuter Brahman
possesses a double nature,
quiescent and active, female and male,
full of gracious thoughts, love and pity.

For Bahai's humankind is the pinnacle of creation,
and whether Western or Asian,
Bahai parent respondents
had a positive view of human nature.
The story we tell about our origin
determines our nature.
Western Christian individualism and introspection,
often ignoring original blessing and royal personhood,
accounts for the more negative view of human nature.
Some even reduced human beings
to naked apes,
while to others they are little less
than angels, co-creators with God.
        It is very difficult
        for those who have a low self-image
        to find authentic self-fulfillment.
        If the result of our research can be generalized,
        it would mean that it is more difficult to bloom
        in a Western Christian context
        than in an African or Asian one.

Did you never think
that you would have been happier and more fulfilled
as a Pagan than as a Christian?
Is that type of envy or nostalgia not an ingredient
in much of Christian literature and reflection?
        Scanning our memories
        we realize
        that those who most often influenced us
        in a positive way are
        the ones who appreciated us positively,
        who appreciated our royal personhood.
        Seeds of glory
        are the birth right of each of us,
        yet too often we are denied
        conditions for germination.
        Too few people bloom.
Glimpsing this royal personhood
people in all cultures and in all ages
sought and related to a beyond:
Tao, Brahman,

Eternal Thou, Supreme Being,
Great Mystery,
Yahweh and Abba.
Even Marxists dreaming of another future
acknowledge a kind of transcendence
and the immense potentiality of human existence.
    Twentieth-century physicists
    to whom the Big Bang appears
    an exquisitely orchestrated affair
    intuit a hidden Principle
    which appears to organize
    the cosmos which reverberates
    through each one of us.
When we realize
the immensity of royal personhood
we appreciate
that we are the blossom from roots
of fifteen and a half billion years of evolution.
    In mysticism we reach
    the deepest ground of our being.
    It is as if our tap-roots have found their spring.
    Our original chord is struck
    as we enter the symphony.
    The most powerful and profound currents
    of people's consciousness converge in mysticism.
When that string is plucked
the whole universe, and all that is "beyond,"
vibrates in us.
An awesome experience
we often hide from each other,
although it is more common
than thought and admitted.

    Contemporary spiritual tendencies
    reflect the shift
    from individual atom to relating wave.
    Native American Indians,
    Buddhists,
    Eastern and Western Christians,
    Sufis, Taoists
    and adherents of African tribal religions

have found each other and convergence
in the creation-centered spiritual tradition
articulated by theologians
like Matthew Fox and Thomas Berry.
The concept of the original blessing of creation
has restored cosmos, eros, and adventure to faith,
and has banished boundaries of doctrine,
exclusiveness and intolerance.
It celebrates an erotic,
playful and compassionate God
in whose image women and men are made.
    As cosmos and woman
    are embraced by man
    in an increasingly holistic
    and ecologically-aware society,
    domination and manipulation are transformed
    to co-operation and participation,
    to a gentling of society.
Not that all this develops
without any hindrance or obstruction.
There are seriously negative aspects
in the world in which we live.
    Our schools continue to teach fragmented "subjects"
    which do not touch the inner sensibilities
    of young people
    who leave school
    insensitive to people, cosmos, and beauty.
Is this worthy of human creatures
who are the unique self-consciousness of the universe?
In which way can each one of us,
a concrescence in the cosmic web,
change the world?
    How can we transpose the vision of unity
    present to a degree
    in non-Western, non-industrialized societies,
    to the whole participatory world?
It is relatively easy to think
of all kinds of human alternatives.
The difficulty is
that they often remain mere utopias.
The danger is that trying to realize them

might reveal their unreal nature,
and their imposition leads to useless violence and terror.
Human history, old and new,
is full of those horrible attempts.
>   What we are thinking of here is not of that nature.
>   The models we are proposing
>   have been and are lived
>   in the peace and harmony of the happy family,
>   the newer nuclear and the older extended ones.

Living in East Africa for many years,
we became aware of tribal peoples
putting first things first:
life, human relationships, and harmony with nature.
Their societies were integrated, their lives full of meaning.
The guy-line of their tribal web was intact,
though threatened externally by invasions and imposition
and internally by the felt need
to break through the limits of their societies.[3]
>   In Western society at large
>   life often appears neither sacred
>   nor worthy of reverence
>   as enormous energy is spent
>   on weapons of mutual destruction;
>   human relationships appear disposable,
>   and human greed rapes the earth.[4]
The universal dimension of our lives is ignored:
as individuals we fragment, polarize, and divide.
We pit complementary ideas against each other:
Christian versus Moslem,
socialism versus individualism,
man versus woman,
the American exclusive belief in liberal capitalism
against the Russian doctrine of state communism,
Thatcher's conservatism against Labour's socialism.
We polarize partisan aspects of reality
as if they are all and everything.
We play society out against the individual,
the individual against society,
the town against the land,
and anima against animus,

falling this way
from one unwholesome exaggeration
into another.
   The world is changing rapidly.
   Homogeneous communities of the past
   are disappearing.
   In one and the same city,
   street, or even apartment building,
   people live in different cultural worlds,
   times, and spaces.
Our relation to the environment
is changing rapidly.
Interpretations of what it means
to be a human being may vary from dwelling to dwelling.
In one and the same house of humanity
there are—thanks be to God—so many rooms.
We have to live together in that one divine house.
We have to allow each other a place on the Tree of Life.
   Though we all know this
   when we are at our best,
   when we are our contemporary selves,
   the ways we think of ourselves
   and educate our offspring
   often only hesitantly live up
   to those new experiences.
At worst, it appears that from technological childbirth
to premature literacy
Western people are preparing
for a no-longer existing world
of dualism, domination, and manipulation.
At best, parents and teachers,
friends of wholeness and integrity
ignite our spark from theirs
and initiate us into the fullness of life.
   It is frequently
   the exploration and celebration of the arts
   that introduces us to the beyond,
   and to a New Creation of compassion
   as all peoples become aware of each other
   and of all dimensions of their being.

Life is enriched in a qualitative leap
from pop music to Beethoven's *Ninth*,
from a Mickey Mouse cartoon to van Gogh's *Sunflowers*,
from a newspaper editorial to Shakespeare's *Hamlet*,
and from fundamentalist religion
to the Bible, Koran, and Bhagavad Gita.
In these reflections we hope to explore
our infinite possibilities
and to stimulate ourselves
to participate in the breakthrough
to another type of world
where fragmentation and division
are overcome
as each of us realizes
that in the cosmic web we are united
with silk and gossamer threads
to every stone,
plant, animal, and person
in our galaxy
and beyond.
>   *Our relationships and possibilities*
>   *are infinite.*
If you don't believe this,
think of the dreams you had when a child,
or take a child
and look into the infinite depth
of its eyes and vision.
>   You are that dream,
>   a divine dream,
>   you are that child
>   a conspiracy of co-existence.

CHAPTER THREE

GATHERING TOGETHER
THOUSANDS OF THREADS

Remember earth breathed you into her
With the air, with the sun's rays,
Laid you in her waters asleep, to dream
With the brown trout among the milfoil roots,
From the substance of star and ocean fashioned you,
At the same source conceived you,
As sun and foliage, fish and stream.

Kathleen Raine

The rhythms of the moon weave together harmonies,
symmetries, analogies and participations
which make up an endless fabric,
a net of invisible threads
which binds together at once humankind
rain, vegetation, fertility, health, animals,
death, regeneration, after life, and more.

Mircea Eliade

In the core of the Trinity
the Father laughs

and gives birth to the Son;
the Son laughs back at the Father
and gives birth to the Spirit.
The Trinity laughs
and gives birth to us.

Meister Eckhart

He was an African artist,
from Africa's and humanity's heartland.
He told how he had loved the old Catholic rites:
the strange repetitive singing,
the incense, the bells, the vestments,
the Latin language
with their mysterious vowels and consonants
in an order and a with a sound,
he had never heard before.
    Then suddenly
    without anyone having been asked
    —as far as he knew—
    that language was changed,
    and so were the rites.
    The priest so beautifully dressed in front
    turned around and spoke the language
    they themselves had always used
    for bread and wine, for salt and oil,
    for water and family.
    To him no new world opened that day,
    and an old one closed down.
    So many connections
    seemed broken and lost.
He said that it reminded him
of the story of that couple
living on the shore of a lake,
who saw every evening the sun go down over an island
some distance from that shore.
The island would light up in orange and blues,
in white and purple, in silver and gold,
and every night they wondered
about that beauty and those riches.

One day they decided to have a closer look.
They built a boat, though it was no more than a raft,
and they moved and sailed over,
to find that the island
was just sand and mud, water and dirt,
like the place they came from.
      It is the same with us.
      Learning and technological skills,
      our "scientific" method,
      have torn us away from the older,
      mysterious world of humanity,
      but also of our own childhood.
That mythological fairy-tale world
has been broken up.
Totality disappeared,
integrity became difficult,
connections got lost.
      In a splitting world you have to betray part of it;
      you can't be faithful to all aspects of reality.
      In a world that is split
      you always destroy something,
      or, worse, someone.

A child is born attuned to the earth,
with perfect pitch and telepathy that peaks at four years.
Things appear full of life:
the sun, because it shines,
the moon, because it grows and shrinks,
stones because they roll and bounce,
the river because it runs, sings, and enjoys doing so.
      Our world remained like that
      —alive and full of spirit—till puberty.
      Like our ancestors we appreciated
      the earth as the living mother
      our astronauts and cosmonauts saw again
      in their momentous glance of earth from space.
When we went to school, still full of wonder,
open to all experience,
and with an innate receptivity for language,
we knew about five thousand words,
and had absorbed

without knowing they were rules
syntax and grammar.
We correlated meaning and sound,
we were full of wonder and sensitivity,
our hearts leaped when they saw
a rainbow in the sky,
snow early in the morning,
a frog jumping in front of us,
or a young dog wagging its tail.

To a happy child, plucked rose-thorns floating
in a stream
are sailing ships bound for the horizon
of a radiant future.
    Myth offers everyone an abundance of images
    to link child and young person
    with the great themes of life.
    Value, order, and society
    are woven together organically.
    Myth offers a glimpse of deep truth,
    at the same time revealing and hiding,
    giving and withholding,
    so that, never satisfied,
    the appetite remains whetted.
Endlessly children will listen to parents and teachers
who tell stories of isolated heroes and heroines,
who mirror the child's predicament.
While listening with wide open eyes,
they realize that they themselves will one day
have to go out into the world to find the treasure,
the fulfillment of their innate potential.
They know and feel
from their own tumult of feelings and intuitions
that not all is good in the world,
that there is evil lurking, too.
    Fairy tales offer light and dark,
    good and evil,
    speaking to the child's conscious and unconscious.
    Adults who appear as selfish giants,
    will one day be transformed,
    and the child realizes

that nature is benign as well as savage,
because in those stories
animals and plants,
the sun and the other stars,
help the hero.
The assurance
that however attractive and powerful
evil might appear,
it will ultimately be overcome by good.
The fairy tale
is necessary
spiritual food for the child.
Do our religious myths not tell
that same story about the light and the dark,
about the light that will overcome?
Would not life be intolerable without that hope,
told and handed down again and again.
Is not that bonding to sun and moon,
to sky and cloud,
to water and grass
to friend and foe
our deepest need?
From the womb the fetus
—aware of the possibilities of tenderness and cruelty—
is in need of a society
which cherishes every pregnant mother,
and through her the delicate fragility of the growing child,
weaving and upholding
the thousands of threads
that binds a child to the world and womb
from which it is born and comes to us.
We have to rediscover in ourselves those threads,
gathering them together again,
before we can pluck those strings,
rebinding us to the world of
the myths and the tales of our youth,
where friends and enemies,
plants and flowers,
animals and spirits, elves and dragons,
divinity and humanity, are interwoven.

Each one of us
drew from the world's primordial matrix,
threads of matter and dream,
with which we wove our life tapestry,
dazzling with color and shade,
with threads sometimes bright, sometimes sombre,
but always complementary and interwoven.
Human tapestries holding
unsuspected richness and fascination,
because each one of us,
is the flower,
the ascending arrow and consciousness
of fifteen and a half billion years of evolution.
For anyone born in this fabric
all is possible.
      Children know this mystery,
      the distance they come from echoes within them,
      they carry the world from which they are born.
That past is in all of us as a dream.
It is the reason that we think of the past
as a golden age,
as lost times,
as far better days and nights.
      It is the reason for homesickness that drives us back
      to the far-off places we are coming from,
      it is the explanation of the nostalgia
      that makes us surround ourselves
      if we can pay the price
      with antiques and old toys
      to get in touch again with those dreams
      of long ago.

Psychiatrists assure us
that many psychological disturbances in later life
originate in the pristine upset of this world.
If the dragon was never killed in the stories we heard,
it threatens us all our lives.
If threads were broken indiscriminately
in that seamless world
disaster will keep threatening.
      We remember a child

growing up in an apartment block
of a rather dreary 1960s town development
no grass, no trees,
only concrete and some shopping malls.
Once, only once, her mother took her to a park.
The child grew almost insane,
like a cow coming for the first time to a meadow
after a stable-winter.
She started to pick grass, leaves, and flowers
in wild abandon.
She collected acorns and branches,
mushrooms and a caterpillar
and wanted to put all that in a box
to bring it home.

Children keep people and things together.
For them all is alive and bound up.
If you pull at one thing
the rest is pulled up with it,
the wheat with the tares.
If you recall one image the whole of reality appears.
      We express this
      also in modern psychological thought:
      children are spontaneously right-brained.
      They feel and think holistically.
      They can do anything.
      They can dance, sing, write poetry,
      and compose music.
      Take the test yourself.
      Ask your youngest child
      to draw your face on a piece of paper,
      and she will start without any further hesitation.
      After a few minutes you will hear
      with the self-assurance of a Rembrandt
      "That is it, here you are."
      But then, suddenly,
      when she is ten or twelve years old
      she cannot draw anymore.
      At least that is what she will say.
      She has become devastatingly constrained
      by what she has "learned," by what is "right."

Their left-brain development stifles them all the time.
It is as if the older world,
where all was kept related and together got lost.
Artists and mystics remain practically the only exceptions
proving all the time
that this *whole world*
lives and thrives,
—although hidden away from most of us.
Detached from our mothers
we all had the innate impulse to relate.
From birth to death our lives are influenced
by relationship with stones, plants, animals,
and most of all, people.
At particular times in a child's life
primary instincts are irrepressible
in their manifestation of eros,
the desire to have friends,
the urge to relate and commingle.
As a child you, too,
must have surged with energy and motivation.
But parents,
teachers and wider society
tend to repress these urges
in the interests of hygiene and conformity,
premature literacy,
and gratification of parental expectations.

Great educators
from Maria Montessori to Alexander S. Neill
have encouraged sensual experience,
the living root to our primordial matrix,
the thread that connects us to the earth's womb
we are all born from.
Cut off we wither,
experience dryness, emptiness
and—to a degree—death of this inherent potential.
The feelings, emotions, and sensations of a child,
—and of ourselves—are the focus of personality,
and deserve respect and nurture.
They also need to be educated
—in the original meanings of that word—

to be drawn forth, to be kept up and supported.
   If denied, a child's openness and trust,
   curiosity and self-esteem
   will diminish, dry up and disappear.
   Denied the opportunity of living their own life
   they will become *as-if* personalities,
   for parents and teachers,
   and finally even for themselves.
Recent research suggests
that aggression and destruction
have a direct link to the repression
and consequent disorganization
of the child's primary instincts.
   Play is another characteristic
   of all healthy young children,
   artists, divergent thinkers, mystics
   and great people in general.
   Picasso called art *noble play*.
In play the imagination transforms the world,
plays around with it,
finds new connections and associations
without a why
and without any sense of urge or reward.
   Play incarnates joy and freedom.
   It has to do with relationship,
   and a continuing reaching beyond,
   a breaking through all existing barriers,
   a falling away of distance and time.
   Mechtilde of Magdeburg,
   the great medieval Rhineland mystic,
   described even God as a *divine playmate*.
   Play is religious,
   because it rebinds the child and us
   with the unity experienced in utero.
   In play one is fully human,
   for self and selfishness are absent.
   In play we are open to primary process thinking,
   and to all experience,
   it is while playing that great ideas are born,
   that discoveries are made,
   that insoluble problems are solved

as in a dream.
Aboriginal people keep this world alive
even in our days.
Some people still intuit this knowledge:
Indians of Brazil believe that the dead turn to water,
and return to the earth as dew to be taken up again.
Each speck of dust
contains Buddhas without number.
Don't your infinite connections leave you breathless?
That is why
to many of their Western contemporaries
they seem wise,
because their childhood world
remained their norm.
  It is the reason why some believe
  that it is only in our contact with their insights
  that our technological wasteland world
  might find its needed healing.
  The only way
  is to look for the loose ends
  all around you,
  the disconnections,
  the short-circuits,
  and reconnect,
  relate again,
  to see things in their context,
  with love as an all binding force.
It is often the older ones among us,
elders and grandparents,
who have found their way back,
who are rebonded again,
who tapped back into the old wisdom
with a spark of refreshed imagination in their eyes,
and the wisdom of age in their hearts and minds.
They often relate best to the young,
telling their grandchildren
about the world in which we all once lived
and solved our problems.
  Dreamland found again,
  integrity and wholeness restored.
  It is through those stories

that we are interwoven with the past.
Neglecting those connections
disintegrates life, meaning, and sense.
 We are not only connected
 through stories and tales
 with all other creatures around us,
 we share protons and cosmic radiation
 from the beginning of time.
 Our mental health and well-being
 is influenced by the rotation of the earth,
 the phases of the moon, the rhythm of the seasons,
 the winds and the waters.
 Our bodily rhythms are linked
 to the cycles of night and day.
 Our matter itself is connected with all around us.
 The protons of your heart
 at one time dwelt in the dust of the stars,
 and maybe in the petal of a flower,
 the wing of a dove,
 the blood of Golgotha,
 or in the heart of a Chinese Mandarin.
Physically and psychically healthy children
play this connection out in another way.
They have an irresistible urge
to get in direct contact with reality.
 They splash in water,
 roll in grass,
 climb trees, taste fruit and dirt,
 smell flowers, and fill all their senses.
This human child
you once were
bouncing and tumbling around,
dreaming and playing,
sensing, feeling, and dancing
was sent to school.
 While earth promises nurture, security,
 and endless possibilities,
 we are too often suddenly torn from it
 and subjected to mechanistic thinking.
Childhood's dynamic participation has to give way to
the manipulation and domination of Earth

as we deal with problems separated from real life.
Precision replaces romance,
our unique biological timetables,
in which we all have our own sensitive periods,
are sacrificed
to a uniform rate of development and achievement.
From school days to employment
disembodied thinking is rewarded
while our emotional and instinctual self shrivels
except, maybe, in some leisure hours,
when we dance and sing, express and create,
make love and relate.
Neither intellectual knowledge
nor gold can compensate our loss.
Why do we allow our children—and ourselves—
to be wrenched from our primordial matrix?
If they cannot feel any more,
they are reduced to stone.
It is their play
their imagination
and cosmic connections,
that holds promise for the future.
That is how it was with us in the beginning,
that is how it should be with us now,
and for all time to come.
Dag Hammarskjöld said:
maturity is the unclouded happiness
of the child at play,
who takes it for granted
that he is one with his playmate.[1]
That is also the reason
why so many of us feel bitterly betrayed
when we see images of starving children in Africa,
child soldiers in Iran,
millions of street children in Asia and South America,
teenage riots in our own inner cities,
together with the simultaneous
exploitation and condemnation
of teenage sexuality.
Their hearts and their heads,
their persons and their potentialities

are as wide as the world,
as wide as the universe,
but it all seems lost.
  Their love could be our joy,
  their insight our redemption,
  yet they are lost to themselves,
  and therefore also lost to us.
The life links of these children are shattered.
A breach that effects us, too,
in an interconnected world.
Each of us is diminished
if one child starves or is psychically scarred for life.
  Their plight symbolizes our unwillingness
  or maybe better our incapacity
  to form community,
  to form the tapestry we are,
  to gather together threads
  that should not be loose;
  to interweave fibers
  that belong together.
  We are, when like children,
  life's longing for self.

CHAPTER FOUR

LIFE'S LONGING FOR ITSELF

Where is the life we have lost in the living?
Where is the wisdom we have lost in knowledge?
T.S. Eliot

The life of the individual...makes history, here alone
do great transformations first take place and the
whole future, the whole history of the world, ulti-
mately springs as an organic summation from these
hidden sources in individuals.
C. Jung

And for all this, nature is never spent;
There lives the dearest freshness deep down things.
Gerard Manley Hopkins

The holy ones of the Earth Tradition are unknown to
white Western society because we train our offspring
to ignore the Earth's great growing spring of beauty
and wisdom, and to concentrate instead on the clerical

and bureaucratic skills necessary to continue and
deepen our assault on the earth.

Brian Swimme

We were driving on a road in Kenya
late in the evening.
From behind us the lights of another car
came nearer and nearer.
The car passed us,
it was driving fast,
too fast for the road
which was not that good.
At any moment a villager
might cross the road.
    A man did pass,
    we could see his shadow
    in the light of the car in front of us.
    The driver of that car saw him too late,
    the car swerved,
    toppled over once, twice
    and landed in a ditch
    at the other side of the road.
We stopped and rushed over,
there were two persons in the car,
a woman and a boy of about ten.
She was bleeding and unconscious
when we arrived,
the child seemed not hurt,
He was screaming hysterically
clinging to the woman:
"Do not die, do not die,
what am I going to do, what am I going to do?"
    Next day in the hospital the woman told his story,
    he was her only child,
    already in a state of shock before the accident,
    because her husband
    had left her a few weeks before.
    That broken life-line had upset the child,
    who had asked her for days and days:

"You are not going to leave me,
are you...?"
The fear of separation ravages our children,
not only because so many divorces of parents
threaten their connections with them
—according to the National Center for Health statistics—
half of U.S. marriages
of 20 and 30 year olds
will end in divorce,
but also because their relations
with non-parental adults are made suspect.
 The National Children's Society in England
 felt obliged to advise in 1987
 that any adult
 treating an unknown child with warmth and kindness
 endangers the life of that child
 by encouraging belief
 in the trustworthiness of adults!
Societal bonds around the child seem to have collapsed.
Even in the most dreadful period of child labor in Britain,
and nowadays in the Americas and South East Asia,
children maintained their links with society.
In the older societies those threads are essential.
In those societies children can look
to their parents, their extended families,
their village and their tribes.
Western children deprived of this breadth in relationships
become consumers at an increasingly early age
of soft toys, games, and fashions,
provided by parents to ease their consciences.
 No wonder that children
 vent their anger against this type of society
 by destroying whole planets in computer games,
 and when older
 by ripping through the upholstery of buses
 and underground trains,
 hurling stones at shore windows,
 wrecking public telephone booths,
 spraying their (admittedly rather artistic) graffiti
 and decorating their bodies
 because they have no other space

to express themselves.
The enormity of this lack of caring
suggests that global society
is abandoning her children,
who consequently see no meaning
in the lack of community.
> In fact there is no place for them.
> There is no real life.
> They acquire self-destructive habits,
> because they are left alone,
> or they dream
> —like Cosette in the Broadway show
> *Les Misérables*—
> of a place,
> where no one is lost, where no one cries,
> of a castle on a cloud, with a lady all in white,
> who loves her very much.
> Today in the full light of our scientific knowledge,
> the whole of humanity is looking for that lady;
> finding her, too, dressed in white,
> our common *Mother Earth*,
> acknowledging her feminine worth and power.

In mythology the abandoned child
often heralds a new moment in history:
Zeus, Romulus and Remus,
Moses, Buddha, and Jesus
were all in one or another sense abandoned.
Despite the worst crimes committed
against humanity and herself,
Anne Frank, a twelve-year-old Jewish girl,
believed that ultimately good would prevail over evil.
It is hope in goodness that makes human life bearable,
and the human person sacred.
> Not only in fairy tales but also in real life,
> angels, elves, and fairies
> are present at the cots of abandoned,
> unbonded children.
> They foretell what is going to happen to them,
> their destiny,
> the new beginnings they are going to make,

the new ways
in which they will bind things together again.
Remember Moses in Egypt, Solomon, Isaiah, Jesus
and so many others.
Notwithstanding their abandonment
angels and prophets indicated
that there was a place for them,
a task, a mission, a reference.
This being bound to meaning was a quality
we often lost.
How often do we not think:
"I did not make of my life,
what it should have been,"
and how often do we not hear the complaint:
"Was I really born for this?"
expressions of the feeling
that we, too, seem to be abandoned,
seem to be lost.
How many of us
can sincerely cry with Gerard Manley Hopkins:
"What I do is me, for this I came!"?
These questions are no longer merely an issue
for the individual.
It is as if whole societies are asking them
in an ever growing identity crisis.
Traditional societies retained an intuitive understanding
of their organic links with life.
People build their own houses, grow their own food,
fetch their own water, birth children on the earth,
and bury their dead in the family compound.
Everyone participates.
No one is so specialized that he or she depends
for building, providing, or healing on others.
They are not surrounded by "experts"
whom we encounter at every decision of our lives.
Birth, puberty, marriage, and death are celebrated
in initiation rituals
linking past, present and future.
Teenage sexuality is encouraged to flower
in fun, exuberance and seriousness,
for sexual potency ensures the continuation of society

the flight of the ascending arrow of life,
the tumbling down through time of the living water.
To give life is a joy to be celebrated,
it is solemnly full of ultimate meaning.

We grew up so differently!
We lost so much,
and though we gained a lot
from a material,
technological, and medical point of view,
and though we should not romanticize the past,
we might ask ourselves whether here, too,
new connections should not be made.
Should not the old thread be interwoven
in the new patterns we found?

Only our beginnings remained the same:
we all grew in the darkness, the moistness,
the warmth and security of our mother's womb.
In utero we evoked our mother's response
and initiated the birth process,
when it was not appropriated by Western medical experts
whose analgesics drug mother and baby
at, arguably, the most important moment of life:
the moment of initial bonding.
What was once reserved for births that caused difficulties,
is now more and more generally used.
If current trends continue, 40 percent of babies in the U.S.
will be delivered by caesarean sections in the year 2000.
Can a mother wholeheartedly relate and welcome a baby,
if she and the child are drugged?
Is the old way, when the mother crouches on the earth
and receives her baby in quiet warmth and gentle light
not preferable, when possible?
Aren't Western blanket and crib
but cold and sterile substitutes?

Otto Rank, the psychologist, suggests
a thing we all know by now:
much psychological disease is a result
of a trauma at birth.
For healthy growth a baby needs

the instant undivided attention of mother or carer
in a sensual and erotic relationship.
In her face
the baby needs to see love and dependence mirrored,
rather then her unconscious needs,
which the baby will be compelled to gratify
at the expense of self-realization.
    It is not new that mothers have to participate
in the economic activities of their society.
In less "developed" countries
mothers have been doing that all the time.
Though mothers in Africa had to work long hours
for their family's survival
babies are carried on her back
and echo her body movements:
when she leans over, they are leaned over;
when she looks around, they look around, too;
and when she dances, so do they.
The modern urban African mother leaves her child home
when she goes to work and cannot pay for a day nursery.
The child is taken care for by a kind of maid, an "ayah,"
most times a young girl from up-country,
who glances occasionally at the baby,
while she is playing in the street for the rest of the day.
The first babies who grew up like that
—in an a-social silence—
came to school
having speech and learning problems.
    Many children go to school or a pre-primary
at the age of three, four, or five.
Despite Plato's almost 2000-year-old anguish
at the effect of the alphabet
on his much older students,
we continue to deliver children prematurely
as we were delivered ourselves
into a world of thirty-six abstract symbols
oblivious that their and our ancestry flows
through animal, plant, stone, star, and galaxy
to the primeval fireball.
Even our human life-links often got lost,
parents and grandparents are our direct link

in the cosmic web, in the tree of life.
We share their blood, we are their genes,
their life and vital force flows mysteriously
on in and through us.
In the older societies naked ritual
re-presents these links
often obscured to the modern child,
living away from the earth
and from the extended human family.
Both poverty and affluence sever these links
at terrific cost to a child's
wholesome psychological and physical functioning.
Traditional child-rearing practices have continued
through the greater part of humankind's evolution,
and maybe you were reared like that, too.
Though not all contemporary Western change
was for the worst,
it is wise to consider
the extent and the result of this change
for today's life,
if only to understand ourselves well.
Children are small,
weak, and emotionally dependent
for many years.
If their needs for love, warmth, shelter,
nourishment, and protection are met,
they grow to full personhood;
if not, they will need to be healed,
that is to say, made whole,
later in life.

Children thirst for an education
of discovery, exuberance, and delight,
and if they experience a growing up of another type,
they will one day realize that it should have been different.
It is not without reason
that retreat and counselling centers
are full of books on healing.
    In his book on education and human culture,
    The Human Cycle,
    the social scientist Colin M. Turnbull

gives a vivid description of how he,
as an English schoolboy,
was not educated in anything concerning sexuality.[1]
The Western teenager is encouraged
to suppress his sexual curiosity
which parents and teachers largely ignore.
They make little reference to puberty,
and, if anything, encourage feelings of guilt,
guilt that one can give life,
guilt that one can pass on to another
that tremendous center of reality one is!
In most traditional societies
the move from one stage of life to another
was dramatized by ritual,
which always embodied some ordeal
as an indication of the harshness one would meet:
male or female circumcision,
an act of bravery,
a tattooing of the skin
or highly symbolic signs like baptism, initiation,
first communion, confirmation, and death rites.
Urban life is for children and adults alike
reduced to a continual "catholic smog"
without end of detergent smells, exhaust fumes,
junk drinks and fast foods,
canned music and cheap thrills.
This supermarket world is further reduced
to two dimensions by television
whose stories and word are accompanied
by ready-made images;
denying children (and adults!)
the possibility of imagining
and creating their own world.
    Child mental illness, adult loneliness,
    teenage suicide and depression
    are the fruit of inadequate child care
    and that type of child abuse
    that is defined as necessary child rearing.
    Society too often protects parents and teachers
    who bend children"for their own good."
    With the negative view on human nature

which we met in our research
as mentioned in chapter two,
all this is inevitable.
Belief in "original blessing"
and the consequent innate goodness
renders harsh child rearing repugnant.
Premature literacy
tears children
from their physical and spiritual matrixes.
It causes the blocks we meet in ourselves as adults
meeting the frightened
and helplessly undeveloped child in us.
May we instead offer our children
an impassioned and spirited education
of play and exuberance of life.
In these times of ever-rising unemployment
our educational system and aims must change.
But the system should
not only change because of that.
The system must also change
to give every human being
in the core of their being
the glory of a well developed child,
for the child is father of the man—and woman!
Young people are presently leaving school
insensitive to people, beauty, and the earth alike.
Should education, to do with cosmos, eros and mythos,
be reduced and trivialized?
Was your education and that of your children
really all it could have been?
   Knowledge is an adventure into the unknown
   not a scaffolding for the future security of a few.
What is, then, the hope for us
to regain threads we might have lost,
or were never bound up with?
Our divine nature herself built in a corrective,
as she so very often does,
in case something fails in us.
   Leisure,
      the joy of God's own seventh day,
      is a gift

even our technological age
did not lose,
and in a certain way
even popularized among us.
It is a time we can spend to re-create self,
to reach from the now of our day
back to the then of the child in us.
We can decorate our home,
with all we missed out on then,
we can plant a garden—even in a can—
and cherish the earth.
One flower in a bottle can transform a slum dwelling.
We can envelop ourselves in myth,
pay attention to our dreams,
love and enjoy, draw and paint, dance and sing,
write poetry and prose, be sad and weep,
fish and play games, be merciful and forgive,
enter in ourselves and meditate, grow food and cook,
have friends and lovers and children;
we can extend and stretch and deepen ourselves
as far and as wide as only a child dares to reach and guess.

> Fortunately there are small communities,
> who have intuited all this even before we did:
> sometimes our old synagogue, church, or temple.
> At other times schools where children
> prepare not only for examinations but for life,
> and churches where one does not only worship
> by praying,
> but by taking care of street children,
> homeless people,
> and where one thinks in terms of
> bringing all together,
> of peace and the needed social transformation.
> There are health centers where conservationists
> are studying medicinal plants
> on which in any case
> still two-thirds of the world depend
> for healing.
> *The leaves of the trees*
> *are for the healing of the nations.*

Creativity and the "eureka" experience,

the finding of paradise lost,
the reconnecting with the child in us,
can only be born from the play of the imagination
which is active only in leisure time.
The English word "school" is derived
from the Greek word for leisure.
The wisdom of the ancient Greeks ensured
that the child within the human being
was not lost until death.
Leisure was the greatest of all goods,
and the leisure of those privileged few
has given us much of what we term "civilization,"
and, to a certain extent
has educated the Western world.

    This ancient Greek attitude
    was initially spoiled
    by Saint Paul's Christian work ethic,
    and later by the Marxist belief
    that a human being is essentially a worker.
    Leisure, as a by-product of technology,
    is often viewed
    as a negative aspect of unemployment.
    Our very value as human beings
    is frequently measured solely by the work we do
    —or do not do.

And yet, we sigh:
Thank God it's Friday!
and city gents turn from chasing stocks and shares
to chasing foxes, deer, and salmon.
We spend loads of money on leisure.
The best paid ones among us
are those who fill our leisure time
which is not always re-creation time,
and in which the imagination is not always revived.

    The happiest people are those
    who organize their life in a way
    that their hobby is their work.
    These people thank God
    not only for Friday
    but for work.
    For them, work, leisure, creation and invention

flow into each other as they did in childhood.
We should go back to find our future.
It is in the past of our own lives
that myth, story, love, music, and art
give us hope in ever present possibilities.
The potentialities of that time,
whether then fulfilled or not,
remained with us in our nostalgia and dreams.
Ideologies and philosophies,
political systems and economic standards,
catechisms and even facts are pale,
sterile and cold in comparison.

Considering human and cosmic destiny
in this lunar age
we must start with, cherish and never lose,
the child who is our parent,
older and wiser than all of us,
as our grandparents know.

CHAPTER FIVE

BORN FROM BLACK EARTH, BLUE SKY, WHITE FIRE, A BREEZE OF AIR, IN FULL LIGHT

One should identify with the universe itself.
Simone Weil

Every part of this earth is sacred to my people
every shining pine needle
every sandy shore
every mist in the dark woods
every clearing and humming insect is holy
in the memory and experience of my people.
The sap which comes through the trees
carries the memories of the red man.
Chief Seattle

how the boys
With dare and downdolphinry and bellbright bodies
huddling out

Are earthworld, airworld, waterworld thorough hurled,
*   all by*
*   turn and turn about*

Gerard Manley Hopkins

My children do
Not go to school.
They will grow up
With the wild trees
Of the bush
And will be burnt down
By the wild fire
Of the droughts!

Okot p'Bitek

It was in Rome during the reign of Pope John XXIII,
a reign that could hardly be called reign at all.
John lived on inspiration,
surprised himself continuously,
and was humility itself.
We were standing with a crowd outside St. Peter's.
There was a rumor that the pope was going to pass.
He did, waving very rotundly from a car window,
with his large papal hat slanting over his head.
One woman in the crowd clapped her hands
and shouted to the bystanders: *Proprio tirato della terra!*
which means: "Really pulled from the earth."
She was speaking of the pope.
She wanted to indicate that he was really a child of the earth,
not someone apparently so aristocratic
that he seemed to come from the heavenly clouds,
like so many popes before and after John.
        Aren't we all born from that same earth?
        Even those who decided to leave their homeland
        in view of a better future,
        still go back to the trees they grew up with,
        the earth they played with and ate from.
It is such an obvious fact that in the womb of our mother

we already led an existence that was a type of vicarious life:
it was the life of plants and animals, of milk and water
of minerals and of the sky
above the place where we lived.

> I am what is not what I was.
> Seeds, trees, and bird, alas!
> Seed, tree, and bird was I![1]

Those who saw their parents till the earth,
sow seeds, collect eggs, pump water,
realized this in a special way, when asked by those parents
to help them to milk the goats and cows, feed the pigs,
pick strawberries and gooseberries,
harvest potatoes, and weed the vegetable patch.
> A dry spell meant less milk,
> a thunderstorm, dirty water,
> a hot summer, dry grass,
> and rain, wet feet.
Our childhood was romance with the cosmos,
eating dirt, testing and tasting everything,
playing mud, chaining daisies, seeking puddles,
picking flowers and spying insects.
> Touch, smell, taste,
> hearing and vision
> tingled with interest,
> joy, freedom, and delight.
We sang reality:
we saw a man in the moon, heard the ocean in a shell,
and saw the sun in a buttercup.
We rejoiced in turtledoves of rhyme and song,
but today we hardly notice a pigeon
until awakened to its presence by our children.
> As we move toward Saint Mark's in Venice,
> the National Gallery in London,
> Saint Peter's in Rome,
> the Capitol in Washington,
> they want to stay and feed the pigeons.
> They prefer to buy bird food,
> rather than put their money in the bank.
They know why we choose to walk

in the forest at weekends,
go to the sea for holidays,
organize picnics,
climb mountains, and dream of cruises.
    Something of all this is kept alive
    in some of us
    when we buy plants, fishes, crystals and stones
    to decorate our homes,
    when we water and feed the life around us.
    In some countries like Japan,
    every educated person keeps in touch
    with this magical life world.
If trees around them have no space
to grow out fully, they grow in miniature,
in a tray,
bonsai trees are no higher than twelve inches,
and sometimes hundreds of years old.
    Don't we all prefer to live in a home,
    surrounded by grass, flowers, trees,
    birds, squirrels,
    not to forget those who surround themselves
    with numerous pets,
    ranging from ants to Great Danes,
    from goldfish to tabby cats,
    from parrots to horses.
We even fake,
and while losing contact with the cosmos,
we fill airports, restaurants, libraries, and our own homes
with plastic plants and artificial flowers
untouched by the creative force of God's hand.
The green dragon,
earthworld, waterworld, and airworld of childhood
have given way to atoms, oxygen and H_2O.
Little wonder that Okot p'Bitek, the East African poet,
rejects for his children Western education,
which denies their organic links with the earth.
His children will follow nature's dynamic cyclical processes
of creation and destruction,
however demanding and painful that might be.

    Pierre Teilhard de Chardin knew this pain:

as a child of six,
he was devastated
to see a cut childhood curl of hair burn
realizing that he was not immortal.
His bitterest tears were shed
when his iron plow hitch rusted.
Many Western children today
lose not only the elements at too early an age,
but also the value of life itself,
in a world around them
obsessed with weapons of death on one side,
while on the other side people die of starvation.
Maybe that is why some young people
wear black
in mourning
for the world that might have been.
Little wonder that many,
have a quick jump at fulfillment
this world does not offer
with over-eating and over-drinking,
and finally often with drugs and alcohol.
They use and abuse
"substance," as we call it,
the substance of this world,
not realizing that "matter"
is related to "mother."
Any other romantic relation
seems to be lost.
In fact those relations are lost
in the competitive and one-sided approach of our world.
This attitude does not only harm them and us physically.
It blocks their learning.
It falsifies the real nature of our knowledge,
even of our scientific knowledge, in the strict sense.
All science is basically a use of metaphors.
A direct access to nature and her processes
is not given to us.
It is always *as if,*
it is always *once, long, long ago.*
Our greatest scientific originators,
scientists and inventors,

knew of this bond.
Isaac Newton said that he did not know
how he appeared to the world,
but to himself he seemed a boy
playing on the seashore diverting himself,
now and then finding a pebble,
while the great ocean of truth
lay undiscovered before him.
Do you remember how he found out about
the law of gravity
when an apple almost fell on his head
while he was having a nap
in a farmer's orchard where he was working
because the university at which he studied
had sent students home because of a cholera threat?
Does not this sound like a fairy tale?
Would Isaac have been able to make that connection
if he had not combined
his scientific mind with that fairy world?

For Alfred North Whitehead,
mathematician and philosopher,
romance is the first step in all learning
to convey the radiance and infinity of possibilities.
Too often the wonder, mystery,
gentleness and excitement of the world
is lost at school.
Fritjof Capra, scientist, author, and mystic,
suggests that we teach in a poetic way,
which is the child's way:
    we tell them about the cosmic dance
    then look at the details.
    We say to them you will have to unlearn
    some of the details later
    so don't believe them too firmly.
    It is just a model.[2]
We should explain
that to understand our splendid universe,
we have invented models,
which are not one hundred percent true,
and which we have to unlearn later on,

if we want to live in the reality we are.
>Were you taught at school
>that our way of looking at things
>is only one of many?
>That we will never be able to express
>in our models and thoughts,
>our wildest imagination and most fantastic dreams
>the fullness of ourselves,
>and of all we are bound together with
>in this world of ours?

Even our noblest expressions of mind and spirit
in literature, music, prayer, and liturgy;
our best political and social theories,
bind us with the food we eat and drink,
and without that food,
without cabbage, potatoes, carrots,
wheat, rice, milk, fat, proteins and vitamins,
calcium, iron, copper, zinc, and especially water,
we would not be able to do anything at all.
>Most of us are aware
>of our protein dependence on animals,
>who in turn depend on plants and grass.

Few of us probably realize
that we also depend on creatures
such as fungus and bacteria,
vultures and earthworms,
who live on the refuse of our community
breaking it down and returning it to soil or water
in forms that are used again
by the primary producers: plants and algae
who influence our climate.
>Every vulture and jackal, every ant and rat,
>contributes to the life cycle.
>Agriculturalists and conservationists
>have realized that they cannot interfere
>in any ecosystem without shaking the whole.

There is growing awareness of stewardship
of the earth and all its creatures.
An awareness others never lost.
The earth self,
the land and the forest

were their body.
All those elements, atoms and molecules,
dance with us,
making our dancing possible.
They sing with us,
enabling us to sing;
they pray with us
in the shine of the warmest mystical light,
sigh with us in the dark of the night of the spirit,
they are with us when we embrace,
preparing for the human future.
Without them
there would be no *Ninth Symphony* by Beethoven,
no prayer like the Our Father,
no painting by Rembrandt,
neither Jesus nor Buddha.
Too often schooling hides this from us.
It does not encompass the *Dance of Creation*
of mystics and twentieth-century physicists alike,
leaving us with *a heap of jarring atoms,*
and an attitude toward the world around
that is not only ungrateful,
but even without any mercy.
Rain forests are cut down,
water levels are allowed to sink,
animals disappear, insects are hated,
and food is wasted.
Brian Swimme, a physicist who works with Matthew Fox,
calls the universe a green dragon,
to remind us that we will never be able to capture it
in language, thought, or symbol.
He writes of the sparkling epiphanies
of earth, air, water, and fire
we so urgently need.
Over fifty years ago
the novelist D. H. Lawrence
wrote about a dragon, too.
He lamented
that we have replaced the divine dragon
of wildness and mystery
with thousands of little serpents or worms.

A relevant reflection today,
when even church leaders
ignore the sins of geocide, biocide, and genocide,
to concentrate on individual sin,
and when schools and parents
are concerned with marks on the leaves of learning,
while the sap of the Tree of Knowledge
is not tasted.
Primal peoples never lost the dragon
—they did not suffer lessons, doctrine and catechism.
Like children, they *taste and see that the Lord is good.*
While ritual constantly re-presents meaning
and reinforces order within their society,
the Western child's guardian angels,
Loving Shepherd,
and the Garden of Eden,
are emasculated,
until only a vague sense of duty, guilt, and confusion
remains,
which most of us know so very well.

Young Masai boys
walk around on their enormous plains,
painted and decorated in hues of ochre
that indicate to them and their society
that they are going to be integrated
into a world
in which they were born
as non-participators.
For them observation
is a matter of life and death,
as beasts of prey are an ever present possibility.
These boys can name
every plant, insect, and animal
in words holding their outstanding traits
and conveying their place in the cosmic order.
The same order was appreciated in the West
three hundred years ago,
when it was realized that all creation was made up
out of the same elements, yet in varying degrees,
from angels to stones.

Non-industrialized peoples
rarely lost respect for their lives.
They do not make weapons
to destroy the earth many times over,
but thank it for the life it gives them.
Forest people acknowledge a duty
to manifest the essence of what they have eaten:
as the ears of the corn they must also be ripe and give life.
    Eating fast foods alone in front of a television screen,
    we miss the conviviality
    of family and community meals;
    we do not suspect the cosmic connections of food,
    which link us to earth, moon, sun, stars,
    the milky way, and galaxies without number.
Every time we drink a cup of coffee or tea,
we are connected with those
who prepare it, who buy it, transport it,
and with those who pick the leaves and berries
somewhere far away on the slopes of Mount Kilimanjaro
in sweat and poverty at the other side of the world.
    Plants, animals, and people die,
    that we might eat and drink.
    Cattle ranchers in Central America and Amazonia
    destroy two and a half million hectares
    of tropical rainforest
    every year,
    grossly degrading another ten million hectares,
    to convert the land for beef cattle
    who, in toto, consume forty percent
    of the world's grains.
    Thus every hastily eaten hamburger
    contributes to the world's protein deficiency,
    and to the willful destruction
    of the living canopy of rain forests.
    Those jungles are put down
    to provide bullocks with the enormous amounts
    of vegetal proteins to produce for us
    some beef ones.
Can we doubt,
or at worst, ignore,
the dignity of plants and animal sacrifice

or of human labor,
and the poor division of our goods?
    The West African statesman and poet,
    Leopold Senghor,
    pointed out years ago
    that Western knowledge of a fruit
    and in fact of everything
    differs essentially from African knowledge.
He said that in Western science
an orange, for example,
will be dissected and sliced so thinly
that it can be observed under a microscope.
It will be smashed and pulverized beyond recognition
until the scientist can look
at the internal structure and composition of a cell.
With that type of approach, practically nothing is left
of what the orange may say of itself:
Look at me, this beautiful orange!
We murder to dissect ,
test animals who suffer our diseases,
not because they got sick,
but because we made them so.
    All this does not mean,
    that the Western approach
    should be stopped,
    though it definitely
    has to be monitored,
    in a more humane way.
The danger is that we overlook
our more original, more traditional relationship.
Science is not only giving us knowledge.
Knowledge is not the only motive we have to be "scientific."
Science helps us to predict the behavior of things,
ourselves included.
Those predictions make it possible
to control, to master, to dominate.
It is that power that might eradicate
—and in fact it does—
our respect for nature around us as a living reality
to which we all belong.
    Science is based on reflection.

Reflection is always a *third* moment,
a *third* that does not make sense
without a *first* and a *second*.
The *first* is our experience,
the real stuff of human life,
the *second* is the story we tell
digesting that experience,
the *third* is our reflection.
An educational policy,
that limits itself to the third,
neither stimulating the second
nor respecting the first,
is simply killing
the human, artistic, and aesthetic approach.
While science investigates,
the arts and religion interpret.
While science gives humanity knowledge and power,
arts and religion give meaning and togetherness.
Life cannot be fragmented.
Look at yourself!
Don't you feel a more whole person
when you give all of yourself?
Aren't you more healthy when you acknowledge
the dark and unconscious in your nature?
Do success and achievement in the world's eye
really fulfill your potential and learning?
Has your understanding of individual and part,
of quantity and measurement, not been at a cost?
Are you still able to feel with your own heart,
see with your own eyes,
and experience with your own body?
Aren't you and others more creative
when you draw from *all* the springs welling up inside you
—pure and impure?
Wholeness is holiness,
holiness is health.
Matthew Fox in his creation theology
recalls the invitation of the German poet
Rainer Maria Rilke,
who invited all of us to *dance the orange*,
the gift of billions of years of cosmic energy

born from black earth, blue sky, white fire,
and a breeze of air, in full light.
And even when all around us
have muddied the clarity
of these relations and realities,
you can make them clear for yourself and live them
remembering that all beauty and life
in animals and plants
is a silent enduring love and yearning.
In that way we will slowly become
more reverent not only towards them,
but also to our own fruitfulness,
to our thinking and feeling
our creating, engendering, and shaping.[3]

Aren't the warmth of a tabby
and the gentleness of a rabbit,
lining their nests with fur from their tummies,
experiences all children should have?
Isn't education to do with
radical amazement
and wonder at the cosmos and her creatures?
To be surprised, to wonder,
is to begin to understand what so many philosophers
from Plato to Ortega y Gasset
have been saying all through time.
    We are glimpsing the cosmos anew!
    The green dragon is waking up!
    The Creator,
    once more the Lover of Creation
    embraces her with a kiss.[4]
    Sky Father and Earth Mother meet.
    Sun, moon, and stars
    shine magic and enchantment again.
    Creation spirituality,
    peace, green
    and inclusive feminine movements
    embrace Mother Earth,
    woman, man, fertility, plants, animals,
        and all peoples.
Life is in the ascendancy;
we have again glimpsed the Woman

clothed in the sun with the moon and the stars at her feet,
because the astronauts the Americans and the Russians,
the Europeans and the Asians did.
Earth appeared as a blue and green
exuberant jewel,
sparkling and translucent
in an otherwise bleak universe.
She is a living organism with no boundaries.
You, too, saw her like that.
You must have seen their pictures of the world
of which you also are a part,
born from its earth,
floating in the blue sky,
   yes you are floating in the blue sky,
on our flying home-planet earth,
shining in the white fire of the sun,
breathing air in the irridescent radiance
of full light.

Let us not only speak about "others."
That is too easy.
What about ourselves?
Consider your world view.
Are you devoted to stone, plant, animal,
people, yourself, and God as Thou,
or do you relate in order to use, dominate,
and manipulate them?
Are you never stopped short in your tracks by nature
have you never been struck
by the beauty of, say, a slice of cabbage,
or did you never cut, see, and cook one?
Do you only hunt or eat animals,
or do they enrich your life, your horizon and perspective?
Cave-dweller artists realized thousands of years ago
that animals are beautiful as well as edible.
Do you have time for everyone,
rich and poor,
black and white,
scientist and mystic,
or are you too busy working?
And if you are busy with those
in your management and business,

are you trying
to get the goods of this earth
well divided between all,
or do you hope to get them or their money value
as much as possible for yourself?
Do you see God becoming
in stone, plant, animal, person, and galaxy?
Do you ever look at the sky and the stars,
at the earth and its worms, at the plants and their flowers,
to find God's joy and color,
laughter, love, pain, and suffering,
growth and decay, beauty and goodness,
or is God
the remote judge
whom you beg to save your life and your soul?
Is your life self a prayer, singing reality,
or is religion imprisoned
in one compartment of a busy individual life,
on a Sunday morning,
or a set of special exercises you do
to be able to pray for an hour or so.
    We suppose that the readers of this book
    take care of themselves,
    in health, food, drink, and physical exercise.
But—how do you relate to the creatures,
you are sharing your planet with?
The plants you have,
your pets, your garden, your jewels.
What is of stone, of wood,
of vegetal or animal material in your house,
like wool, cotton, paper,
or even that oil product, plastic.
    Trace them all to their natural sources.
    Think of how you are connected through them
    to the fields, the sky, the moon and her cycles,
    the oceans, the seas, the mountains,
    the sun and his fire.
    Even the paper you are reading this from
    connects you directly
    to a forest in Canada, Finland, or Sweden,
    with its animals, its insects, its earth;

and the ink on this page
does the same
to minute fossils of marine origin,
who millions and millions of years ago,
were growing and mating,
breathing, living, dying, and fossilizing.
In this type of *I-Thou* relationship,
with earth and other,
each of us is a focus
of caring, sharing, relating.
We might know this, we might not.
If we don't we will never realize ourselves.
We will not be able to celebrate
our inter-connectedness either.
We might become a danger
not only to things we relate to,
but to ourselves, too.
A relatedness that should be celebrated.
    In this way we might appreciate
    Teilhard de Chardin's vision of the Eucharist,
    that means *thanksgiving:*
    the altar is the cosmos,
    the bread is the harvest
    of plant, animal, human and divine toil,
    and the wine is the sap of earth's fruitfulness
    wrung from cosmic suffering.
All is offered at each sunrise by the whole of creation
as fire penetrates every new day.
Earth, fire, water join in elemental union.
We have found the cosmos—and ourselves,
our origin and substance,
being ourselves,
because of our connection
with the All.

CHAPTER SIX

RAPT IN EROTIC LOVE

God with honour hang your head,
Groom, and grace you, bride, your bed
With lissome scions, sweet scions,
Out of hallowed bodies bred.

Gerard Manley Hopkins

How beautiful are you, my Beloved, and how delightful!
All green is our bed.
How delicious your love,
more delicious than wine!
How fragrant your perfumes,
more fragrant than all other spices!
Your lips, my promised one,
distill wild honey.

Song of Songs

For indeed at what moment do lovers come into the
most complete possession of themselves if not when
they say they are lost in one another.... And why
should not what is daily achieved on a small scale be
repeated one day on worldwide dimensions?

Pierre Teilhard de Chardin

Attraction is rooted in the deepest depth of life.
It is the primal energy of the Universe.
An emotion,
a movement toward harmony and accord,
toward the oneness that was lost.
It is the desire
that is the core self
of our heart.
> Once, long, long ago
> all belonged together;
> *one,*
> not united,
> as we had never been divided.
Unknown, but being all truth;
unloved, but being love self.
> Do you remember that mysterious story
> about *Adam*
> the original human being,
> about how bored *it* was;
> alive, that is true,
> but without dynamism,
> without creativity;
> relating to *adama*, Mother Earth,
> surrounded by a world,
> taken up in it, even naming it,
> but alone, without any taste for it.
Then this *it* was divided into a *she* and a *he*,
and attraction, dance and song,
music and taste, perfume and embrace,
love, life and offspring began.
> Once we belonged together.
> We still do.
> Human memories and hope
> link past, present and future,
> while peak moments allow a glimpse
> of the Eternal Now,
> the infinite present each child still knows,
> and we only remember.

Love-making in the biblical tradition
has to do with wine, and perfume,

spice and honey, lilies and apples,
raisins and cakes, with gazelles,
frankincense and myrrh, music, glad songs,
endlessly sweet words, fountains and winds,
honeycombs and doves, budding vines, pomegranates,
candlelight, a cloud of incense, storms, torrents,
and divinity Self.
    All these are bound and pulling together,
    when in the Song of Songs
    the lovers embrace.
    Not only man and woman
    are then brought together,
    but the whole of creation with them,
    to complete and fulfil herself.
When love ignites being and arouses passion
boundaries fall away,
and embracing, we rise for a moment
from this world,
having a *pré-experience*
of our risen state,
before the general resurrection of the flesh,
as a French philosopher, Jean Guitton, aged 84,
recently said.[1]
And the Greek Church Father, Saint John Climacus,
would have agreed.
    This loving union is next to life
    Creation's greatest gift to humankind,
    God's gift self.
    We don't need
    anybody's permission to marry;
    it was God who gave that permission
    once and for all.
Church and school banishing the erotic
to the pornographic scene
bled themselves of spark, flame, vitality, and life force.
They forget that the derivation of be*lief* is *love*
and that of *truth*: be*troth*al, a promise of love.
No wonder that young people,
and older ones young at heart,
find these institutions alienating and suffocating
the spark within.

When family, school, church,
youth and the erotic
part company,
self-discipline, dynamism, and gentleness
lose each other.
Life looses its coherence and zest,
and the young, denied vibrancy,
turn to the energy of pop and rock.
Wouldn't you? Don't you?
If there were no attraction,
galaxies would fly apart,
the twinkle of stars would disappear,
the earth would disintegrate,
lovers would love no more,
the human family would fall asunder.
Relation is the integrity of the world.
Everything is fulfilled
and completed through everything else.
Energy passes from one organism to another
along foodchains which are linked together
in complex food webs
with many branches and connections.
Sun, moon and stars are involved.
Plants convert to chemical energy
about one percent of the sun's radiant energy
that falls on them.
This is sufficient to produce 120 billion metric tons
of new organic material each year !
After centuries, we speak once more,
of Brother Sun and Sister Moon,
of Sister Water and Brother Fire,
and see the Universe
like some people and children do,
as a communion and a community,
not romantically,
but as a scientific fact.[2]
This old and new child-earth relationship,
often crudely ruptured at home and school,
is not recovered until the young adults
once again delighting
in each other's body and spirit,

in dance, song, and play,
in eating and drinking together,
in wine, perfume,
roses, gemstones,
in the stars and the moonlight,
are breast to breast with their lover.
Old and sacred literature
is full of human relations
with the fruits of the earth:
we are asked to bloom as a flower,
to grow as seed, to be clear like water,
to be tasty as salt, to be wise like a snake,
humble as a dove and strong as a lion.
The fatted calf is sought in the fields
for the prodigal son.
Oil is poured over feet, massaged with hands
and dried with hair.
Bread and fishes are gathered in the plains
for multitudes of people,
and again and again people sit together
at breakfasts and suppers, at cookouts and picnics,
with bread, fish, oil, and wine.

We still feast at birthday parties,
weddings and other celebrations
relating to the same things.
In a way those feasts are even
more wonderful and cosmic than the older ones:
with tea from India, coffee from Kenya,
fruit from New Zealand, cheese from Holland,
pears from Japan, and wine from California.
Yet in another way
supermarket availability and layers of packaging
have removed us from earth.
Vegetables have every scrap of earth washed away,
and really fresh foods are difficult to find.

The memories of the old relations are still there:
the pang of satisfaction and lost longing
for self-grown vegetables, our own tomatoes,
home-baked bread, grandmother's cookies,
home-made wine, pure cotton, linen, and wool.
We suffer when inorganic connections

and distribution systems related to money
replace our earthly links.
The most intimate part of the environment
to which we relate is our very own body,
in school and family too often an embarrassment
and relegated to the gym, the games field,
and the bathroom.
Later in life our attitudes range
from excessive cosseting to a technological approach
which manipulates the body to its limits
with work and drugs and endless workouts and jogging.

Do you respect your body?
Do you love it?
Do you oil and massage, decorate and dress it,
because you really love it ?
Do you take into account its biological rhythm,
its own natural time,
so different from the rhythm and the time
we impose upon it, our body,
in view of our self-esteem, our glory,
and the making of money.
The way we treat our bodies
their anxieties, hunger, thirst, pain, anger,
upset, sickness, tiredness and sadness,
but also their joy and pleasure
reflects to some extent how we will treat others.
If we nurture, respect, and sincerely love
our physical selves,
if we accept the "shadows" of our desires and emotions,
of indispositions and failures, of growing up and old,
of being spirit yet in flesh,
we will accept the same in others.

If we ignore or try to suppress
these emotions and tendencies,
if we do not integrate them,
we do not live in the truth about ourselves,
we don't love the ones we are,
we are people of a lie.
We will not develop full relationships
when those shadows and lies fester and erupt
in increasing intolerance for the others' shortcomings,

which we are unable to accept in ourselves.
We will not even be able to believe that others love us,
because we do not love ourselves.
  We can love the other to the extent
  that we love ourselves,
  that is why we should first and foremost develop
  a good and wholesome erotic relation to self.
  A necessary step
  is the acceptance of our doubleness.
  God cut the pair of us
  from one human flesh and spirit,
  anima and *animus;*
  the feminine and the masculine
  complement each other in all of us.
  Not finding this treasure in self,
  how would we be able to find it in the other?
Too often this treasure was not found, the pearl was lost.
Things went wrong, and indeed, they often did.
  It is not without reason,
  that in spiritual centers
  books and courses, seminars and workshops,
  workouts and support groups on healing abound.
It was in those very centers
that relations were misunderstood,
that wounds were inflicted,
and people were hurt.
  We were too often told
  that life on earth was finite,
  incomplete and sinful,
  and not the real thing.
  Instead of seeing ourselves
  as full of possibilities, truth, value,
  and beauty, too,
  we were too often taught to mistrust
  and to examine ourselves endlessly
  in order to distinguish reality and illusion.
We continue our present journey
shaping our lives with attitudes and values
developed from childhood.
The words of the past
ring long in our ears.

We all began when new connections were made,
genes and molecules, cells and electrons,
spinning and chasing each other.
Undulations, oscillations, and vibrations
produced a movement, a coalescence,
a union together, and new life was created,
a new song of harmony sung:
You are welcome.
We love you,
words on which we depended
from the very beginning
and all life through.
Words like a thunderclap, laughing through chaos
and causing the cosmos.[3]
"In the Beginning was the Word."[4]
Was there a word like that at the beginning
of each of us ?
      The Hebrew word *dabhar*
      is dynamic, playful,
      a living creative force,
      and when not spoken,
      the silence of disconnected chaos.

It is mutual attraction, gestures,
and words spoken
that bind mother and child.
      If that bonding is frustrated,
      the insecure and fearful child,
      might spend its life seeking
      to experience and to hear them.
Connection and deep meaning
the indication of old attraction,
reside in language.
      Mother, matter, and material
      derive from the latin *matrix*—womb.
      Derivations indicate significant and startling
      earthly roots and relationships:
      humility has to do with *humus,*—earth;
      and holiness with *wholeness*
      devotedly bound up with all.
      What implications!

Words are living buds on stems
which return us to the generative power
of their roots and original seed.
  Paolo Freire,
  one of the most effective
  of twentieth-century educators,
  appreciates this word-power
  —for him a word is reflection and action
  in radical interaction:
  "to speak a true word is to transform the world."[5]
Words keep us together and break us apart,
they suffuse the whole of our lives,
they are its warp and its woof.
Words should be treated
with the greatest care.
  Amerindians teach children not to speak their names
  as they may be stolen,
  and if name goes, identity goes.
  That is why prisoners are reduced to a number
  —24601—on admission.
Every word we utter
gives authority to some and impotence to others.
Totalitarian regimes know that word-power
and imprison the writers,
who remember the old myths
and the fairy tales of love, freedom, and rights.
Religious communities
based on unilateral authority structures
forbid from teaching those who use different words
or who return to the roots of the same words.
Words, stems, and roots are potent,
they are enticing, seducing, tempting, alluring,
and changing you.
  It is good to think back to the people
  who changed your life in a growing way.
  In some way The Word
  I love you, I will you,
  you are welcome,
  resounds behind their words.
They touched you.
They entered into true dialogue

in which we complete and fulfill ourselves.
Listening and responding
we began to learn who we really are.
>We opened ourselves to their warmth and truth,
>we bathed ourselves in their words
>of love and affection.

The spark within us cannot shine on its own;
it has to be found and named by the other.
>Don't we all know from own experience the story
>of a boy or girl,
>who thought nothing of themselves,
>considered themselves dull and flat,
>shallow and empty, thoughtless and lacking,
>pimpled and ugly, too big or too small,
>who suddenly met others who spoke those words,
>words so sweet,
>that it changed the person
>they had always seen in their mirrors
>and heard in their speech.

Why is it that some do this and not others ?
Faith and hope in the goodness and possibilities
of nature and humankind
are prerequisite to engaging in this dialogue.
>Personal contact
>is the *sine qua non* of teaching
>in many traditions.

Too often people's lives seem
full of textbook language
devoid of conviviality, color and beauty,
awe and mystery.
>Sacred literature, fairy tales and myth,
>poetry and song,
>take second place in school and home.

In pre-industrial societies language has to do
with communion and bonding.
Information is shared, wisdom cumulated.
Inner meaning is hidden
in riddles, proverbs, songs and stories.
The listeners have to discover their meaning
from *within* themselves.

We remember the day an African teacher explained
the difference between the Western way
of telling a story and the African way.
He said:
"After telling the story, you explain it,
you draw moralizing conclusions,
stealing conscience and insight away
from your listeners.
We just tell the story,
and leave the rest to the dynamics
of the story and the listener."
As people moved to towns,
individualism grew,
and social binding weakened,
many of the old stories got lost,
connections fell away,
and a new language, new stories ,
that would bind us together again,
—now at a much larger scale than ever before—
are not readily found.
      Language came
      to divide and separate:
      she is black, he is yellow,
      he is a man, she is a woman,
      she is a Moslem, he is a Jew,
      he is Catholic, she is "nothing,"
      she is conservative, he is liberal,
      and that is only a dog, an insect,
      a plant or a stone....
      In that way anyone and anything
      can be dismissed.
      In those words evolved a world
      that separated the divine from the earth.
      the Creator from the created,
      the light from the dark,
      the masculine from the feminine,
      the heavens from the earth,
      the sacred from the profane,
      inner space from outer space,
      one human group from another,
      the individual from the community,

the "master" from the "servant,"
the "priest" from the "lay" people
one species from another;
a world of dualisms,
hierarchy, dominance, classes,
apartheid, racism, tribalism,
egoism, colonialism.
We must know those others,
we must give in to the feeling
of the relatedness of the whole of the universe,
before we can love and know ourselves as we are.
We have to know ourselves
before we can transform the world.
Socrates, Philo the Jew, Paracelsus, Swami Ramdas,
Mohammed, Lao-Tzu, and Shakespeare
all advised the same.

That human relationship does not just "happen"
is evident from a recent opinion poll
in the United Kingdom,
in which eighty percent of respondents
perceived the U.K. as a place
where *every man is for himself,* [6]
looking forward to a future
at once "dismal, depressing, and frightening."
There is another reason for this sad outlook
on our future togetherness.
We seem to have replaced our cosmic and human
relationships with inorganic connections
related to money.
As E.F. Schumacher noted,
something can be considered
immoral, ugly, soul-destroying,
degrading or a threat to peace,
but until you have shown it
to be *uneconomic,*
you have not really questioned
its right to exist.[7]
Little wonder that the value we place on money
destroys so many relationships,
turning us into "fetishists,"

centering on "gold," on a thing
instead of life.
  It will be a difficult road to reconnect,
  to know oneself, to turn around.
  It is road we have to go,
  it is a travel we have to make.
We are as necessary to each other
as food and water.
We know and feel this.
That attraction cannot be denied.
We do not need to know about sacred literature,
that is full of relationships between sky, earth, plant,
animal, and person
to feel that attraction—that love—
in our body and blood, in our heart and head.
  Myth suggests that the primal relationship
  was between Sky Father and Earth Mother,
  who together birthed creation and people.
  Holy communion for some,
  dialogue and love-making for others,
  incarnate this union of heaven and earth
  at every moment in the world.
Naked together, heart to heart,
lovers lose all boundaries,
as male and female complete each other,
finding themselves.
I and Thou are one.
Initial separation proved after all,
a link.
Each finds integrity through the energy of the other
in peak moments undreamed of.
Sense and spirit are awakened and filled
as the human body is cherished
in all his and her beauty.
  Reality sings in harmony
  as the cosmic self is realized.
  The world gathers herself
  in the consciousness of lovers.
  Creation finds its source and its meaning.
  Eros, the desire to relate
  and to reach out to, is incarnate.

Yet how many people in our society
experience such relationship?
How many turn rather to the non-human,
to learning, magic and religion,
for relief from their human condition.
　　There is altogether too much suffering in a world
　　that apparently neither knows
　　where it is going,
　　nor what it should be doing.
　　Is it not a fact throughout our lives
　　that competition, survival of the fittest,
　　hierarchical authority, violence,
　　ruthless independence, judgmental attitudes,
　　and belief in a distant God
　　hinders us in our relationships.
Our enormous expenditure on weapons,
—handicapping and killing millions of people
as there is less money available
for health, education, and other social services—
arises because we are split
and cannot trust each other.
　　Our *thanatos syndrome*,
　　love of killing and death,
　　must be replaced
　　by that deeper instinct in us:
　　eros.
When Robert Oppenheimer
participated at the first experiment
with atomic weapons,
a phrase from the Bhagavad Gita
came into his mind:
"I am become death, the shatterer of the worlds."
　　It is evident that the shattering
　　first occurs in the human mind.
　　The armament race,
　　—the preparation for mutual assured destruction—
　　undermines life's hope in us.
　　In general, Western societies do not formally nurture
　　loving relationships,
　　they are anti-creational,
　　though most of the youth

sing another song, the one of love,
"We are the world!"

Pierre Teilhard de Chardin
believed that when the world discovers
the energy of love
it will have discovered fire
a second time.
> How can we account
> for that irresistible instinct in our hearts
> which leads us towards unity
> whenever and in whatever direction
> our passions are stirred?
> A sense of the universe,
> a sense of all,
> the nostalgia that seizes us
> when confronted with nature, beauty, music
> —these seem to be an expectation and awareness
> of a Great Presence.
> Leaving the "mystics" and their commentators apart,
> how has psychology been able
> so consistently to ignore
> this fundamental vibration
> whose ring can be heard by ever practised ear
> at the basis,
> or rather at the summit,
> of every great emotion?
> Resonance to the All
> —the keynote of pure poetry and pure religion.
> Once again:
> what does this phenomenon,
> which is born with thought and grows with it,
> reveal
> if not a deep accord
> between two realities that seek each other;
> the severed particle which trembles
> at the approach of "the rest."[8]
Conditions need to be changed.
If wealth was distributed more fairly,
we could be the *one* we are.
> If self-esteem did not depend on economic status

life and giving life would be respected.
If men and women were educated
for wholeness
stress would decrease
and child-rearing would be considered
a privileged experience for both parents and community.
   In these conditions relationships
   would develop and deepen,
   we would be growing
   to the full stature of the human being,
   sometimes called Christ,
   the anointed one.[9]
And what of our schools?
Were you fortunate to attend schools where
cooperation, dialogue, respect, and interdependence
were fostered?
   Or was your school a place
   where children of only one race,
   one nationality, or one religion felt at home?
Those schools no longer seem appropriate
to a global society, a planetary civilization,
a world *oecumene*, a post-industrial communications era,
an ecological age.
   So many children
   in our schools
   have as a special friend
   a child from another culture.
Are these friends going to grow up
and hurt each other
without the intervention
of social or cultural prejudice?
   Diversity is richness and excitement
   —man with woman, black with white,
   scientist with mystic.
   It is the in-between, the relationship, the bond,
   the reference to a common inner ground,
   that generates energy,
   making us, open and empty,
   pure and "catholic," cosmic and universal.
   Attraction pulls,
   but fear of the unknown

holds back.
Pierre Teilhard de Chardin suggested
that the ecstasy of human love-making
can be transposed to a universal key
to birth a world of integrity,
where the Eternal Truth
is recognized in every person
and every created thing:[10]
heaven, earth, and humanity
caught up once again
in the one reality
we all together form,
dressed in the seamless garment
woven together in love. [11]

CHAPTER SEVEN

ECHOING WITH MYSTERY

I have desired to go
Where springs not fail
O thou Lord, send my roots rain.

Gerard Manley Hopkins

A sunset is glorious but it dwarfs humanity and be-
longs to the general flow of nature. A million sunsets
will not spur on men towards civilization. It requires
art to evoke into consciousness the finite perceptions
which lie ready for human achievement. Thus, in its
broadest sense, art is civilization. For civilization is
nothing other than the unremitting aim at the major
perfections of harmony.

A.N. Whitehead

Thou takest the pen—and the line dances,
Thou takest the flute—and the notes shimmer,
Thou takest the brush—and the colours sing,
So all things have meaning and beauty
in that space beyond time where thou art.
How, then, can I hold back anything from Thee?

Dag Hammarskjöld

The greatest tragedy in theology in the past three cen-
turies has been the divorce of the theologian from the
poet, the dancer, the musician, the painter, the drama-
tist, the actress and the movie-maker.

M. D. Chenu

Okot P' Bitek sings his song
    "Listen Ocol, my old friend.
    The ways of your ancestors
    Are good,
    Their customs are solid
    And not hollow
    They are not thin, not easily breakable
    They cannot be blown away
    By the winds
    Because their roots reach deep into this soil."[1]
He became one of East Africa's most authentic poetic voices.
His books sold in tens of thousands,
they were dramatized, translated in many languages,
read over the radio and quoted in cultural gatherings.
    Once he was a small child in an African village
    where a cathedral was built,
    and missionaries settled
    to change the ways of the villagers,
    trying to shake their roots.
Okot's grandparents and parents
forbade him to go to that church,
they did not want his, and their, roots shaken,
but that refusal made the church
even more mysterious to the small boy,
passing now and then
its enormous carved wooden doors,
in a place where doors had never been needed at all.
    One evening, when the bells were tolling,
    and light shimmering through windows,
    the attraction of mystery became too much.
    He sneaked away from home,
    stood for a moment
    in front of those doors,

waited until someone passed through,
then slipped in through the opening
that was slowly closing up again.
He remained in the dark at the back of the cathedral
that seemed to him the house of a giant.
He saw candle lights,
a strange someone fantastically dressed
in blazing colors,
surrounded by children,
who seemed to be white-dressed spirits;
he heard singing in a strange, almost arhythmic, chant,
the same tune repeated again and again,
the ringing of tiny bells;
he smelled blue smoke coming from a small fire
someone was swinging around in a golden pot,
a very heady perfume;
and then the someone in front together with the other spirits,
started to dance, very slowly, and very solemnly,
bending his head and his back,
his arms and his legs,
going up and coming down,
going up again.
    The main dancer,
    put an extra beautiful cloth
    around his shoulders,
    took something in gold from above him,
    suddenly turned around,
    and made with that something in his hands
    with in its center a bright white dot,
    a very wide gesture,
    while the blue smoke went up and up,
    and everyone fell on their knees.
The music and singing stopped;
everyone became so mysteriously silent,
—except those golden bells—
that he could not stand it any more.
He suddenly understood
why he was not allowed to go
behind those heavy doors.
He was in the spirit world, he was with the living dead,
he was in the netherworld, he was with his ancestors,

he was with gods and God, he was in his deepest self.
Suddenly caught by fear,
he pushed himself through those heavy doors,
ran home as fast as he could,
glad to be alive again.

    Okot finished his story:
    "I carried that experience with me
    for the rest of my life,
    because I felt and knew
    that what I had seen, smelled, and heard
    was really in me,
    I had met my deepest inner
    African rooted Self
    behind that enormous set of doors."

Our Mother Earth is dappled all over
with temples and churches, sanctuaries and tabernacles,
shrines and synagogues, mosques and pagodas,
domes and pinnacles, chapels and oratories.
They are her oldest and newest,
richest and most elegant,
her most austere and sweetest,
most visited and best preserved,
works of art and buildings.
In many cases they are the only remaining expression
of lost civilizations and cultures.

    Any visiting alien from space
    would be struck first by those expressions
    of our human genius, our imagination
    expressed in and shining through matter.
    Just like we earth children ourselves
    are struck when visiting far off places,
    entering doors to sacred spaces,
    with filtered light,
    colored windows,
    vivid paintings, buxom sculptures
    perfumes and smells,
    sounds and rituals,
    sacrifices and blessings,
    catching eternity herself,
    who mirrors to us

—whether we are
consciously aware of it
or not—
our deepest inner self.
Voices get softer, a sacred hush is heard,
bodies don more clothing,
gestures and postures flow forth,
many sit or even kneel
for a moment of reminiscence and nostalgia,
prayer and recollection.
    Temple gates and church doors,
    entrances to sacred caves,
    paths leading to mountain shrines or sacred coves,
    are entries to the mystery of self,
    the quiet breath from which all jubilance springs.
Often nature herself,
touches our innermost selves:
his body, *her* body, *our* body,
stillness of a summer evening,
blue-black liquidity of a pond,
mystery of dancing flames,
splash of a waterfall,
clear air on a mountain top,
eternally recurring ocean,
sun bleached beach,
orchid beauty,
sound of a flute-playing child
from far, far, far away.
    It might be a painting or sculpture,
    kept in a building
    almost as solemn as a temple;
    or a piece of music,
    a hymn or a song played in a concert hall,
    or sung in the open
    under the blue of the sky,
    in the heat vibrations of the sun,
    on a hot Sunday afternoon in summer.
And we close our eyes, we regulate our breathing,
hearing the sound of nature or music
as a mantra,
seeing shape and color

as a mandala,
perfume and incense
awakening all we are ourselves
eternity, humanity, and divinity
suffused with the rhythm that animates all,
vibrations of color and sound,
smell, form, and shapes,
moving and swaying:
dancing, it all makes sense dancing and relating together.
As T. S. Eliot so beautifully said:
"In the stillness
there is only the dance."
Humankind's first intuition of life as a whole
was communicated through dance.
Is it not as if the newborn child
with its waving feet, arms and legs,
wide open eyes, nose and ears
is trying to attune itself
to the vibrations of the pervasive universal rhythms?
The whirling of the Sufis,
the Hindu Shiva with many outstretched arms,
Jesus the Lord of the Dance,
African and all dancing,
are religious in essence.
They spring from the source and rhythm of life
inviting everyone to vibrate to the primal rhythm.
Chinese harmony was birthed in dance;
Isthar, goddess of Nineveh, danced;
Osiris and Isis danced;
and Zeus' birthday heralded dance.[2]
The angels tumbled
dancing from heaven
above Bethlehem
All our body cells dance.
When theologians,
—the old ones, the real ones, the Greek ones—
meditated upon Jesus' revelation to us
that God is community, that God is not alone,
that God is family,
that God is not isolated, that God is not aloof,
haughty or unsociable, that God relates,

that God loves, that God is *one*,
yes, but *many*, too;
neither sitting alone on a throne
nor hard like a diamond, cold like a crystal,
majestic like a dictatorial ruler,
they intuited God
as a *life-process*, a parent and child,
and their love in-between,
a loving loved lover,
doubly loving doubly loved lovers,
because that is what it means,
Trinity.
They tried also to find out,
"What do they do,
those three in one?"
They found the answer and they used a Greek word,
a beautiful one, like the name of a child,
epichoresis,
which means
dance.
They are dancing hand in hand,
three in one, enjoying each other,
enjoying their lives.
    If that is true, and if we are their children,
    it should be true of us, too.
    Their dance
    is their kingdom, power, and glory,
    and it should be
    our kingdom, power, and glory, too.
    If that is true,
    dancing is the core of their divine
    and our human nature!
    Only some of our contemporary theologians
    are in tune with this dance.
They have moved
from an absolute immovable Father God
to the wholeness of a loving Trinity
—*epichoresis*—
as the source of life.
    No wonder that
    from Japanese to Amerindian peoples,

from Papuans to Russians
people danced when they began to relate
to each other, their environment
and the unknown.
Isn't that what we all do,
when someone like a pope or guru arrives?
Don't you imagine heaven
as music and dancing,
merrymaking and singing?
   We know a person, who regained consciousness
   after a serious operation,
   while Christmas carols
   were sung in his hospital ward.
   He took quite some persuading
   that he had not awoken in heaven!
Without a whisper of the echo
of that mystery and its music in us,
we are—individually and collectively—
adrift and disconnected.
   It is the vital road to the inner center,
   where mystery, wholeness and attraction,
   art and beauty,
   have their home.

Sometimes it seems that religion and mysticism,
art and beauty are fragile and fleeting in their existence,
yet they are *God's imagination at work in us,*
and no existence has proved more powerful.
   What you feel then
   is not something only yours,
   only subjective,
   it is "impersonal," testable and provable,
   you have it with the whole of humankind,
   it is intersubjective,
   the common source that binds us all.[3]
   It energizes our soul which can no longer be caught,
   empowering us
   to protect the same potentiality in others.
We delight in artists,
like those who transform
sand, salt, and ashes to stained glass windows.

Marc Chagall reveals the dynamism of living form:
brilliant colors sparkle and glow
in a biological way.
    He takes us into ourselves,
    with a beauty hardly known
    in modern shopping malls full of naive gadgetry.
People in all religions have been patrons of the arts.
Cathedrals, mosques, temples, and synagogues
bear witness to the discovery of our inner selves.
    Like religion, art tries to give form
    to a mystery, to faith.
Susanne Langer describes art
as the creation of forms symbolic of human feeling.[4]
They are the dynamic essence of life
which is never still and resembles divine nature
and the essential "matter"
of twentieth-century atomic physicists:
a particle which is a wave,
dancing and bouncing about.
Matter and life are one in a cosmic web.
    Appealing to imagination and intuition
    both religion and art seek to give meaning,
    to express the infinite.
    Our lives are embroidered
    on a background of meaning.
    We need religion and ritual.
Even the most rational of organizations
 —the army, university and big business—
invent formal and informal ritual,
interviews and initiations, promotions and demotions,
parties and jubilees, awards and medals.
We are not so different from *primitive* peoples
only covering ourselves with a superficial,
but sometimes oh so transparent, veneer of sophistication.
    Many of us unconsciously crave
    the mystery and echo
    of vivid and magic images of our childhood.
    We search for myth, metaphor and symbol,
    intuitively knowing that art,
    —analogous to sunshine in the physical world—
    will brighten and enhance our lives

    with clear visions,
    presently hidden from our muddy perception.
Art selects the essential from reality
and makes it speak, sing and dance.
Acknowledging no boundaries
the artistic approach is synthetic and whole
and approaches holiness.
    An artist has always known
    what physicists have just realized
    and mystics have always felt
    that in an interconnected world
    we are not observers but participators.
    Michelangelo did not transform the marble to David,
    he saw David in the marble.
While love completes and fulfils us as people,
art unites us with the creative cosmic process.
It is to do with wholeness, healthiness,
holiness, and healing.
People find that the artist within
empowers them to transcend dichotomies
and clears their vision for radical amazement.
They start drinking from their very own wells,
just as they did
when playing, dancing, singing,
enjoying and imagining life
as children,
becoming conscious of their own potential,
our transforming powers, their own imagination.
    This *conscientization,*
    —as some would call it—
    is a real liberation,
    a powerful instrument for moral good,
    and for energizing change.
That is why lay, and religious, regimes
fear and hate it.
Authors, philosophers and theologians,
who use their imagination, and free ours,
are dangerous to any totalitarian regime.
    In rightist South Africa,
    in leftist-ruled regions,
    but also in religious contexts

they are often banned and ostracized.
The founder of Christianity, Jesus,
—according to religious leaders of his time
an amateur and charlatan—
was a similar embarrassment
to those authorities.

    In our days Pierre Teilhard de Chardin, Hans Küng,
    Leonardo Boff
    were forbidden to teach;
    Boris Pasternak and Aleksander Solzhenitsyn
    had to leave their country;
    Meister Eckhart is still condemned,
    and Matthew Fox is silenced by the Vatican.
    They moved beyond authority to mystery.

Music awakens us to our mystical dimension.
Everyday-time dissolves in Dream-time.
We dwell in music as the artist dwells in his creation
and the dancer in her dance.
Convention is suspended
our deepest depths are plumbed.

    As we said before,
    when a small child
    our personality structure
    resembled that of the artist.
    We constantly revealed our mystical dimension
    in innumerable questions
    which sought meaning;
    and we nurtured it
    delighting in illustration, song, dance,
    music, fairy tale and myth
    which included us
    in life's vitality, dreams and hopes.
Listen to the questions young children ask:
Where do I come from?
and the answer they give.

    They are attuned to mystery,
    even if their parents, school and church,
    blocked access to it long ago.
    Where do they get it from?
    Indeed, where are they coming from?

Where do you come from?
As children we lived reality
against a background of mystery.
And even today
our books, pictures, music and dreams,
now and then, lift us to a higher reality
not above but deep in us.
Children's art reveals their closeness
to primordial consciousness.
To the age of six years, regardless of culture,
their art is remarkably similar.
Human potential seems to have a common source.
    Art is an affirmation of the life process,
        which reveals the significant
        in a biological, organic I-Thou way
    as it enhances our lives
    with diverse memories of lullaby,
        nursery rhyme, story,
        rocking horses, teddy bears, dolls,
        delicate porcelain,
        velvet cushions,
        incense-filled churches,
        fountains and processions.
When family, church, school, and politics
conspire to keep religion and art
dammed up at the periphery of life
society is condemned to live in its void.
    Creative potential wilts,
    "experts" flourish, passivity is the general order.
    People flounder, lose their vision
    and clutch at any straws as they try to relieve
    their deep longing and lingering childhood hope
    that all will be well,
        buying things,
        surrounding themselves with toys,
        that will never satisfy their yearning.
A recent study in the United States suggests
that only ten percent of people over forty years of age
are "creative,"
compared with eighty percent of six year olds.[5]
In the U.K. the average person spends three days a year

in amateur music and dance,
compared to ten days at the cinema
and twenty-four days betting.[6]
    If children are born artists
    why do so many appear to lose these potentialities,
    even their mystical ones?
    As human nature is not responsible,
    it appears that childrearing and education are.
Young people are more
exposed to paintings, sculpture and music of others
than encouraged to create their own.
    To consciously make a mark
    on a blank piece of paper requires faith.
    It is a step in the unknown,
    —did you ever see the face of a child
    who does this for the first time?
    The second mark brings relationship,
    and in due course
    each mark finds its proper relation:
    thus masterpieces are born.
They are too often losing the art of seeing life
with their own eyes.
They are rarely encouraged to create
or develop vision.
School days hardly ever
nurture the need for fantasy and the beyond.
    School, church and family too often neglected
    harmony, rhythm, and beauty
    leaving a child instead with a parts mentality
    and a belief in the over-riding importance
    of literacy and numeracy which,
    —while important skills—
    are never the whole.
Shakespeare cannot be reduced
to words, syntax or grammar,
and neither can you.
A child cannot *light up* without reference
to its inmost life.

Connection with our divine origin
relation with our celestial sources

and potentialities should not be lost.
    We heard even more prayers said by others,
    than introductions to the possibility
    of an inner journey to the sacred mystery
    of our own peaceful self.
Churches and religious leaders
reduced prayer to something
that was their speciality.
They still organize their liturgies in ways
that rarely make you sparkle and vibrate
with the spirit and the source of life within you.
    The gospel stories could only have been told
    by communities that sang and danced,
    ate and drank,
    when celebrating the past, the present
    and the brilliancy of time to come.
    That common and simple meal
    left by that God-signed person Jesus
    to symbolize how we all belong together,
    in a community of loving companions,
    was caught in the straight-jacket
    of a hierarchical priesthood,
    carefully reserved for some.
    Jesus' common breaking of bread
    and drinking of wine,
    became a heavy-handed power structure,
    a parody of what it was meant to be,
    creating separation instead of communion,
    keeping some in, and all the others out.
Like the arts, prayer was marginalized
in the lives of most of us.
It was something for a few chosen and called ones,
making the difference between professional and lay.
    It was as if religious leadership
    was afraid, that once all of us gained access
    to God, to our own inner core,
    their authority and power would fall away.
Excessive ritual, heavily manipulated by priests,
dwelt too much on God *out there.*
Humanity's deepest inner core
was trapped in traditional,

set, and controlled themes:
Annunciation, Adoration, Crucifixion,
Resurrection, and Ascension—
it was as if all had happened already
to others
and we hardly counted.
  Although ritual must be regularized
  for the portentous moments
  of human birth, marriage, ordination, and death,
  excessive ritual bars the road to the God *within.*
Passivity and proxy experience,
rote learning and empty ritual,
too often deny to mysticism and art
the possibility of raising civilization
as they grow and spiral
within and through everyone.
We sometimes don't even suspect
our latent power.
  Once upon a time
  there was the old prisoner we all are.
  He used to shake his bars and wish he could get out
  into the world that was rightfully his,
  but the bars were strong
  and his wish futile.
  One morning,
  an exceptionally beautiful sunny morning,
  rays of sunshine and bird song filled his cell.
  He stirred in utter wonder,
  he felt he could escape,
  though he did not know
  where that feeling came from,
  from without, or from within?
  He got up from his infested blanket,
  walked to the barred door and...
  to his utter surprise opened it.
  He walked down corridors and stairs
  into a brilliant world.
  The prison doors,
  he thought others had closed
  had never been locked,
  but he had never tried them.[7]

Pieter Mondriaan, the Dutch painter,
best known for the abstract gridwork
that divides his paintings like jail bars
explained his work as an attempt to escape,
to the unity of cosmic dualities
and to religious symmetry
which undergirds the material universe.
He wrote that the hallmark of the new age
would be a human
who can live only in the atmosphere
of the universal.

> All of us, made in the image of God,
> are like that old prisoner,
> or like the child,
> told that she could not sing,
> shut away from her song never sung,
> listening only to others.

Somewhere we have lost the way,
for Western education was founded on a rich heritage
of art, poetry, myth, music, and dance.
Plato advised—though only for some, namely the best—
a literary education that began with myth,
which Aristotle considered essential for wisdom.
For Plato, myth and art bring
an instinct of relationship,
grace to the body
and nobility to the mind.[8]

> There are signs of hope,
> some are striving to change the world
> through personal and school philosophies
> based on the sacred nature of each human being
> and the unanimity of humankind.
> The celebration of the arts
> at the heart of the curriculum
> empowers children
> to become integrated and whole personalities
> during a school experience of delight.[9]
> It is unlikely
> that these children
> will grow into adults
> who fill their recreation time
> passively.

Even today many people sensitive to the arts
are more likely to visit gallery and concert hall
than put brush to canvas or bow to instrument.
  This—possibly true of our own lives too—
  is the result of
  educational policies
  which in their neglect of the arts
  fail to draw forth young people's potentialities
  of intelligence and feeling.
Too many educational systems teach us to mistrust
our own experiences,
when they bring us beyond, beneath, above,
the day-to-day world.

In primal hunting and gathering societies
in less technologically developed countries,
person and artist were inseparable,
as they often remain in non-industrialized societies
today.
  Where mass production
  has not banished the craftsperson
  art is woven in the tapestry of life.
  Youths of fourteen years not only provide
  food and drink,
  but also make bow and arrow,
  boat and fishing line, house,
  and their decoration,
  fireplaces and cooking pots.
Art is everywhere—in baskets, carvings,
arrows, body painting, singing and dancing.
  Few Western people think of themselves
  as artists,
  few are able to help themselves
  with life's essentials,
  although we all have this capacity
  however hidden it may be.
Sharing dance, song and craft
from various parts of the world
we grow in understanding and fascination
for those different from ourselves.
  Today's problems, new problems,

require new solutions
—creative responses.
Nowhere are young people
more encouraged in this than in art.
We live in times of rapid change
in increasingly multi-cultural societies.
But how many people really suspect
the richness of diverse cultures and beliefs?
Arts are vital to this process,
incarnating culture and tradition.
Go to Durham, Chartres,
Varanasi, or Isfahan.
You probably have artifacts
from never-forgotten holidays at your home.
Whether you perform or enjoy the arts
you participate in the culture they represent,
and become a more whole person,
realizing not only what you have and give,
but also what you need and receive.
Art is the daughter of the divine,
the Muse is to do with God's Spirit,
and as that Spirit is in you,
you can meet her, freely and joyfully,
by trying to attune
the vibration and rhythm of your body
with your deepest Self.
You can do it by praying
meditating upon a work of art,
maybe an Eastern icon,
or a sculpted pieta.
Relax, concentrate, and contemplate.
Through the senses,
you will reach your inner core.
Only imagination and intuition
will birth a new world,
reveal the mystic, unlock God,
in each one of us
and society around.
Our lives will be rich
in experience and full of meaning.
Boundaries will dissolve in mystery;

the Way back is found.
　　We will again feel and know,
　　as we felt and knew
　　once upon a time in childhood,
　　—before we began to forget—
　　that all peoples and all Creation
　　were born to live together happily ever after,
　　and that things have not to be as they are now.
　　We will dance forever and ever
　　even through death to life.
　　Isn't the whole of life a dance in the direction
　　of the fulfillment that awaits us,
　　where all together,
　　no separation
　　will bar us any more?

CHAPTER EIGHT

WELLSPRING TO OTHERS

Everything, every person, every event, every moment of time is wrapped in a shell. Sometimes the shell opens from within, sometimes it needs help, Shekinah is released. The Shekina in everything, every person, event and moment of time. Sometimes he is seen, sometimes we are invited to open the shell and release his presence in the world. We share in His redemptive process.

Abraham Josue Heschel

When you weed out the darnel you might pull up the wheat with it. Let them both grow until the harvest.

Jesus

Within each soul is a knight who rides out to adventure. But each soul is also a virgin who can receive the individuality of another in true social understanding. And each soul is a battleground where dragons would imprison the soul in prejudice and transform the knight into a self-centered entrepreneur.

John Davy

*All men cannot be outstanding... yet all men, through
knowledge of superior humanness, could know what it
means to be a human being and they do have a contri-
bution to make. It is magnificent to become as human a
being as one is able.*

Catherine Roberts

Not so very long ago in a place
where transport was difficult
and money scarce
—there are many places like that—
there was a maternity clinic.
Many of the babies born left with their mothers
almost immediately after the unbinding of birth,
and the rebonding of mouth and nipple,
eyes and face, nose and smell,
sound and ear, tongue and taste,
skin and warm stroking hands,
nicely cuddled and warm, kissed and admired.
    Some had to stay after their mothers left
    for one reason or another.
    Those babies were visited,
    and the mothers who lived nearby
    did that more often than those that lived farther away.
Those nearer did not only cuddle their children,
feed and treat them, they also took care
—with a friendly word here and an innocent bribe there—
that their children were in a better place,
near the window, the sun, the sky,
the trees, the birds and the earth.
In the dark corners and near the walls
were those less cuddled, hardly—if ever—kissed,
far away from kith and kin.
A nurse discovered, what you might have already guessed,
that those abandoned ones never smiled,
were smelly and grim, and even hardly grew.
A meeting was called, a consultation held,
and a nurse appointed to take the ones in the corners
out in the open, now and then, cuddling and kissing,

talking and cooing endlessly to them
and—of course—they started to smile and to grow.
    Another story, equally true:
    she is a headmistress in an African town,
    —but it could have happened anywhere.
    She noticed that one boy did not feel at home,
    neither with the boys nor with the girls.
    He seemed not to come to himself,
    he did not play, he did not pay attention,
    it was as if he was always just somewhere
    in between.
    She had noticed behavior like that before,
    and did what she had done more often before.
She called for the parents of the boy,
she told them what she had seen,
and she asked the father, do you ever go out with him,
do you ever talk with him, do you ever treat him as a boy?
The answer did not come, so she knew,
and she said, take him with you to a football match,
take him out with you, show him who he is.
    He did, she knew he did,
    because after the very next weekend,
    that son was a different boy
    in class and school.
The Mayan proverb says that
mother is to hold the child close
so that he knows it is his world
and—at the same time—father is to take him
to the top of the highest hill so that he may see
what his world is like:
full of human relationships
that require love and adventure
to become a new wellspring of life.
    You need the other
    as much as a piece of bread;
    the other needs you
    as much as a glass of water
    or —maybe—wine.
At the beginning of your life a woman's eyes,
hands, body and voice
awakened your senses,

and she in turn had been awakened
by the eyes, the hands, the body and the voice of a man,
to be the life-giver to you, another wellspring of life,
not only giving birth to you from her womb,
but also by her touch, her smells and her sound,
her stroking your body from top to toe,
and her smile, telling you:
    You are there! [1]
    Cradled in her hands you cried out your glory,
    your first sucking noises,
    your first "a" and your first "b,"
    your first signs of communicated life,
    beginning in total trust,
    at the dawn of reason,
    to fulfill your human vocation.
Each child born of mother and father
should be sprung into a new source,
a fountain of living water gushing forth
every drop reflecting the whole,
giving freshness and moisture,
life and bloom, color, shape and taste
to all and everything
plant, animal, and human.
A center of life,
a fountain,
children splash in it,
elders sit around it,
women and men carry water home from it,
to drink, to clean, to baptize,
to make merry,
to wash newly-born life,
and in the end
to cleanse the body
before it is returned
to the womb of the earth again.
    It dazzle-breaks the light
    in rainbows of colors,
    it dances in the wind,
    and with its ever sounding music and rhythm
    higher and lower, up and down,
    to the left and to the right, forward and backward,

it even offers shelter against the clamor
and noise of modern life.
Thrusting upwards with an energy of its own,
it draws its water and its energy
from all over the universe,
secretly connected to underground streams
filling up from rivers and lakes,
interlinked with the sky and the clouds
full of steamy, evaporated water,
and falling down in rain and storms,
or much more subtly as softly as dew and snow.
The life in our body, should be that fountain
in which each cell, despite its function,
reflects the whole of our life;
our genetic memory,
our connections with ancestors and the beginning,
with stars and sky, minerals and plants,
animals, human history, work and development,
past, present, and future,
the whole of the community coming together
in that one life-point, that large living cell,
the one I am, relating to all.
"I relate,
and therefore I am."
Are you such a fountain
secure at source,
life giving, interconnecting
with everything and everybody,
always aiming higher and wider,
reflecting the "wholeness" you are
in your life, words and action?
Societal and global integrity
depend on the realization of individual integrity.
If world integrity depends on personal integrity,
we must relate to know ourselves.
"The deeper I go into myself
as an individual,
the more I find my commonness
with other individuals."[2]
If we do not love the world,
if fantasy and daydream do not constantly reveal

horizons of liquid possibility,
if we do not—to an extent—tame and embrace
the dragon of wildness and mystery,
we are not whole and will not have the capacity
to fulfill ourselves and "others"
in relationship.
Consciousness, passions,
earthiness, and mystery
must unite in each of us.
I am the center of the universe,
it is the responsibility I carry:
the shepherd of it all,
You and I, the one shepherd,
of that enormous flock.
You are not alone, I am not alone.
The others around us are the center, too,
like you, together with you,
it is together that we are the world.
It is only together
that we are this world.
that we are humanity.

In an inter-connected world we cannot take
our responsibilities lightly.
Through others we complete ourselves.
St. Paul already noted that together we are one,
members of one another.
We are not just juxtaposed, we are interlocking,
we are complementary sexually, culturally, professionally,
even religiously.
The Christian incarnational idea
of God's immanence,
is offset by the Muslim's confession
of God's exclusive transcendence.
The Christian joy of being saved,
—glorifying in the Messiah, who came—
is tempered by the Judaic experience of the contrary,
when they were caught in the horrors of holocaust,
together with so many others.
The uniqueness of Jesus,
and the ecstasy of being in his company,

makes Hindus wonder about the God-sent saints
they know and experience.
Our self-centered religious desire:
"One thing I have desired, the Lord!"
makes Buddhists ask whether that desire is not
the cause of our problems.[3]
And does not every contact with a primal belief
make us wonder about hearths and virtues,
dances and rites, methods and patterns,
and the early soul of ourselves,
now overlooked?
Wasn't all that we now consider non-Western,
once Western?
What one developed, remained undeveloped in another.
Each specialization, every particular growth,
each inspiration and insight, every feeling and emotion,
casts its shadow.
The dentist knows about your teeth,
and maybe not even about all,
because she is not specialized
in wisdom teeth.
The painter paints,
and the composer composes;
the trumpet player plays the trumpet,
and not the drum;
the cook cooks,
and the waiter serves.
     The modern development of individualism,
     left the social in the dark,
     while the organization of the social dimension
     was often at the cost
     of personal individualism.
It is only together
that we form
the human being,
the willed *one*,
the intended *one*,
the anointed *one*,
the Christos *one*,
Christ!
     Relationship is healing—contact is life-giving.

In full relationship
we actualize human potential
losing,
but at the same time
finding
ourselves in each "other."
It is that intimacy that will bring us
to our fulfilled self,
to final resurrection in spirit and flesh
in body and soul.
To re-establish this relationship,
as old as humanity,
with all and everybody,
is not easy for us,
who are modern in our self-appreciation,
likeable, kind, well-intentioned,
never wicked,
but so deeply and so righteously
absorbed in ourselves
that we have hardly any time for others,
except when they play some role in our lives.
Even looking at a dying starved child
on the screen of our television,
is a thrill and makes
—or does not make—
for our entertainment.
Our "selves" get in the way whether we relate as parent,
child, sibling, neighbor, student, workmate
lover or fellow worshiper.
That those "others" are like the "selves" we are
is not only a reason for radical amazement
but for outright panic, too.
They are not only "others," they are competitors,
they are out to get us, they are enemies,
they are unreliable, they are
our darkness and our shadows,
they are like dragons against which we have carefully
reared and trained ours.
It was not without reason that the first nuclear scientists
called the awesome power of the formidable plutonium core
of their bomb the "dragon."

Our every word and action speaks volumes,
on whether we accept the world where it is
—the status quo—
or work at the one we know it to be.
Do we respect and nurture
royal personhood in ourselves
and in others,
not only paying reverence to our spirit,
but also to the body we are
and have together.
Have we tamed our dragons
of panic, fear, and aggression,
managing to live the fullness of life?
Do we work tirelessly so that the greatest communal
twentieth-century hope-killing monsters—
our armies, navies, and air forces
with all their weapons of destruction, murder,
and death—may be dismantled?
The dragons are many.

There are the cosmic ones
that threaten the survival of life on earth,
in a development that is not sustainable,
and that undermines the earth's regenerative systems
to replenish its soil, water and forests,
and to maintain the chemical cycles.
Forests are depleted, climates affected,
soils eroded, carbon dioxide accumulated,
ozone-layer destroyed,
and the consequent heating up makes the ice melt
to the point that shorelines are threatened everywhere.
There are the more homely dragons,
some of which seemed already domesticated.
In England, for example, thousands of people are homeless
while nearly three-fourths of a million houses lie empty.
We cringe at the management of the world's household:
millions starve as butter mountains rise,
wheat rots in silos, and lakes of milk overflow.
One-parent families struggle for survival
unable to leap out of the poverty cycle.
One in three dwellers in Third World cities

is affected by dysentery, asthma, rickets,
or some equally debilitating sickness,
caused by pollution and inadequate sanitation,
while others live in rampant luxury.
Little wonder that fewer old people see visions
and that even fewer young people dream dreams.

    Denied love and adventure
    families, schools, and churches are falling apart.
    The struggle for survival and achievement
    erodes family life.
    Old people are banished from the family
    while children are abused
    as society washes its hands
    at what goes on behind locked doors.
Socio-economic inequity further dictates
that some areas are for one "class" and "race" only.
Apart and separate we cannot be
a wellspring for others.

    Yet everyday reality is too often
    readily accepted without question
    and alternative constructs not imagined.
    If they are,
    their originators are labelled "trouble makers."
    It is uncomfortable to rock the boat,
    too many people
    are afraid to lose their comfortable position.
Many of us, in the race for achievement and work,
manifest little love and even less adventure,
while our institutions, states, schools
and even "respectable" churches
appear lacking in compassion and love
as the neediest are excluded almost everywhere.
Stale smelling, shabby people are not welcomed
anywhere with open arms.
We confine ourselves to a group of people
be it family, school, church, or workplace,
although we know that life depends
on *all* participating in processes of decision making,
debate, choice, and cooperative effort.
As society appears to polarize increasingly
with the rich becoming richer and the poor poorer,

what can we do to be a wellspring for others?
    Reading newspapers, journals, and periodicals,
    listening to the radio, watching television,
    or talking with friends
    everyone longs to participate in healing the world,
    even those who gave up long ago,
    curled up as they are in the small circles
    of their owned locked-off selves.
Were you never struck by your own compassion?
You must have given in to its dynamics in you
so often, again and again.
    Did you never feel that you had to protect yourself
    against that vibration in you, since it might force you
    to reach out, to be a wellspring of life?
And you closed your eyes,
wishing not to see, not to know, not to feel,
not to hear, not to smell, not to touch
—hiding from the truth about yourself.
You opened neither your heart nor your mind,
and certainly not your door.
    You imagined and lived in a dream world
    where your compassion would not be necessary,
    but you remained alive in the world
    where you felt and knew it is.
You turned away from "others," escaping from the truth
that we belong together,
because it is in that oneness that compassion locates herself.
    "How is it possible
    that suffering
    that is neither my own nor of my concern
    should immediately affect me
    as though it were my own,
    and with such force
    that it moves me to action?"
    In his essay, *On the Foundation of Morality,*
    Schopenhauer answers his own question.[4]
    "I have to some extent
    identified myself with the other
    and therewith removed for the moment
    the barrier between the 'I' and the 'Not-I.'"[5]
If we want to live faithful to ourselves;

if we are looking in good faith for the real ones we are,
if we do not want to live in perpetual frustration,
in fear and worry,
 —blood pressure up
spirit down—
creating in ourselves the breeding ground
for all kinds of disease,
we should try to be the ones we are.

If you bring forth what is within you,
what you bring forth will save you.
If you do not bring forth what is within you,
what you do not bring forth will destroy you.[6]

It is no good to live the one you are not,
it is no good to refuse to be the one you are.
If we are not whole people relationships will suffer
and we will not have the capacity
to be wellsprings for others.
Bearing all this in mind we must nurture
the humanity of ourselves and "others'"
remembering that each is diminished
by the "others'" loss.
 Our authority will spring
 from the kind of people we are.
 It appears that the more humane,
 empathic and sensitive a person is,
 with a sense of humor
 and the capacity to laugh and to weep,
 the more she or he is able to develop
 growth-giving relationships.
 People with faith in the ultimate goodness
 of "others" and the world inspire these same feelings,
 and therefore,
 hope in those with whom they are in contact.[7]
With love and a sense of adventure
life is transformed.
That is why creation spirituality groups,
who return to the source of Original Blessing
(*and God saw that it was good*)
are a wellspring for so many people.

If we are nonjudgmental
our glance will be inclusive
and we grow and benefit
from the richness of diversity.
Human contact
is the depth and the summit of existence.
We must know our place in the human tapestry.
To be open to others we must acknowledge
our cosmic/earth/human connectiveness,
and share a convivial passion for humanity,
that organic web in which every point
is connected to, and—in a sense—contains,
every other point.
Humanity is glorious!
Secure at source,
like the fountain we took as our metaphor
we will allow glimpses of our true selves,
original and passionate.
A bloodless, safe existence is not life.
Our spark from the Divine Fire will ignite
the inherent human spark in all people.
Who guessed what would follow
from Gandhi's march to the sea,
from Florence Nightingale's concern,
from Martin Luther King, Jr.'s, dream,
from Sister Teresa's vision?
People like them imagine,
and in turn create another reality.
The action that followed their example,
did not derive from debate,
conflict, majority rule
or commands of a hierarchy.
It came from a spontaneous emerging order.[8]
Human example is the greatest teacher.
It addresses the immanent potential
of each and every human being.
Our imagination and our unflinching effort
can gradually change the situation.
Why is it that less than one percent of the population
appear to actualize this inherent potential for good?
Abraham Maslow, psychologist,

suggests that one reason
so few reach their full potential
is the loss of heroes and heroines.[9]
There appear to be no adequate substitutes
for the saints, the knight, and poet of days gone by.
Myth, legend, Bible story, and poetry
can presently take second place
to indiscriminate television viewing
with all that this implies.
Few of us do not experience
a pang of longing for Dream time
and children are forever fascinated by those
who share the wisdom of their experience:
the grandparents' and elders' role.
Confining the elderly to old people's homes,
we deny grandchildren in particular
and young people in general
their accumulated memories, experience, and wisdom.
Little wonder that young people today sing:
"I need a hero!
I am holding out for a hero."
We have replaced these heroes
with the anemic substitute
of the well-adjusted person.

Maslow suggests examples
not of well-adjusted,
but of self-actualized people:
Albert Einstein, Spinoza, Aldous Huxley,
Thomas More, Goethe, Martin Buber,
Pablo Casals, and Walt Whitman,
suggesting that they viewed life clearly,
not allowing their wishes and hopes
to distort their view.
They were interested in people, science,
music, art, politics and philosophy
—all to do with harmony and wholeness.
They retained an essentially child-like quality:
they transposed their creative,
primary process thinking to a mature key.
They had a vision, a vocation, for which they lived

and their work, while demanding, was exciting
and merged into play.
They were spontaneous, flexible, and adventurous,
unafraid of making mistakes,
and independent of the judgment of others.
They loved beauty and life,
and believed in a meaningful universe and spiritual life.
All of them had touched within themselves
the universal self,
the feeling and insight one has to have
before one can be a wellspring for others.
They all had their moments when barriers fell away,
in love-making, holy communion, aesthetic inspiration,
an overall vision, a feeling of being one with it all.

    It is a scientist, a biologist,
    who indicates another way,
    to pluck the thread you are,
    to know and feel your connection to the whole cloth,
    and the self-giving well-willingness it demands:
    "...if you want to hear
    the whole mind working at once,
    put on the St. Matthew Passion
    and turn the volume up all the way.
    This is the whole central nervous system
    of human beings,
    all at once.[10]

It is something,
you might be able to do just now!
How much more powerful
is such a mind-blowing experience
than pages and pages of information.
Arts bring the sense of hope, and promised adventure
to complete fulfillment.
Beauty, harmony and unity,
essential to personal integrity,
yet denied to so many people groping for the wholeness
they consequently cannot reach,
are the calling and privilege,
the passion and pain of the artist.
Poets, musicians, mystics, and artists of all sorts,
have—through the ages—expressed the vision

that the whole of the world is mirrored and kept together
in each grain of sand, blade of grass
or musical phrase.
Our vision is broadened if we are bound up
with all around us.
    At once deeper and higher
    than personal achievement,
    enthusiasm is the inner creative impulse,
    the youthful freshness of spirit,
    which reveals the artist within each of us.
    It inspires "others" with faith
    to wander in the world
    and energizes them to cast aside
    and re-create
    an unacceptable, exclusive reality
    into an ever more just one in spirit and flesh.
Each of us has the awesome responsibility of educating
—drawing forth and supporting—
those with whom we come into contact,
especially those born from us,
those who will be the new shoots on the old tree,
nearer to the sun and the roots
than all those who ever were before.
We have the power to create or destroy
our fellow human beings.
If in family, school, church and workplace,
we encourage wholeness and integrity
each person will be empowered
with the unquenchable energy of a wellspring
—a wellspring for all those "others"
be they mineral, vegetable, animal or human being.
If achieved on a universal scale
truth, beauty, and justice will embrace a unified planet,
the whole human being,
in which we all find our fullness,
—so often called *heaven*—
and will be the wellspring self.

CHAPTER NINE

DISCREETLY WITHHOLDING

Friendship is a miracle by which a person consents to view from a certain distance, and without coming any nearer, the very being who is as necessary to him as food.

Simone Weil

Only great pain, the long slow pain that takes its time...impels us to descend to our ultimate depth....I doubt that such pain makes us 'better'; but I know it makes us more profound... In the end, lest what is important remains unsaid: from such abysses, from such severe sickness, one returns newborn, having shed one's skin... with merrier senses, with a second dangerous innocence in joy, more childlike and yet a hundred times subtler than one has ever been before.

Friedrich Nietzsche

Throughout the whole of life one must continue to learn to live, and what will amaze you even more, throughout life one must learn to die.

Seneca

Love winter when the plant says nothing.
                              Thomas Merton

It was during a tutorial on a very hot afternoon,
at Nairobi University in Kenya, in the heart of Africa.
The topic had turned and turned time and time again,
and at a certain moment we were discussing,
death and life after death.
Then one student said,
"As you know once you are dead
you are without a shadow."
        And though we had our doubts
        on whether a dead body
        really does not cast a shadow,
        a serious point had been made:
        as long as we live,
        we will live with our shadow
        and at death the shadow will fall away.
        Darkness, negativity, will disappear
        at the moment that we are one,
        reconnected with it all.
Shades are there,
because of my build,
because of my height,
because of my development and growth.
They are there not only bodily,
but also psychologically and spiritually.
        Living in the West,
        living in Europe or North America,
        you and I developed our private personality
        to the extent that
        when we are projected in the full light of day,
        our social dimensions
        remain in the shade,
        less developed, underdeveloped,
        or maybe undeveloped.
        Some even go so far as to say,
        that we even have neither the language,
        nor the imagery,

to express ourselves in that social dimension.
Competition, acquisitiveness and aggression,
evident to an increasing extent
in the "Westerworld,"
work directly against community and society,
yet competitiveness and beating our neighbor
are often introduced early in school life.
In other continents and regions
others developed their social dimension to the point,
that their private personality,
seems to remain hidden in the darkness
of their communal being.
We seem to be each other's shadow.
What we developed so specially,
was not developed as specially by them.
And the same is true the other way round
When White meets Black,when Black meets White,
when East meets West, when West meets East,
when North meets South, when South meets North,
when anima meets animus,
when man meets woman,
that shadow play is there,
all the time, in language and talk,
in myth and story, in social structure,
politics, economy, and religion.
You may—afraid of the dark side in you—
try to escape your very own shadows
repressing them, only paying attention to the light in you,
developing it out of any proportion, glorifying it,
wallowing in its growth, hallowing your own light,
getting bigger and bigger, richer and richer,
brighter and brighter,
a swelling parasiting and vegetating on the rest,
devouring all you can find,
growing into a malignant tumor, a cancer,
and finally a death threat to yourself and all others.
It is that light you should moderate,
the brightening you should withhold,
so that your shadows do not thicken
into utter and fatal darkness.
It is in those dark shadows,

that new growth should begin,
it is in those shades
that our failures hide.
> The seed grows in the earth,
> the child develops in the womb
> in darkness pregnant with mystery and hope;
> the scientist tries to unfold
> what is not yet known;
> the traveler penetrates the regions
> left blank on his map;
> the mystic enters the darkness of night and soul
> to find some illumination.
It is from the dark that our hearts beat
their endless life giving rhythms.
It is from the dark that new life is born.
Yet we shun darkness and shadow,
somber places, feelings, pain, suffering, silence,
our own blind spots,
and—most dreaded of all—death.
> Life, mineral, vegetable, and animal,
> is to do with light and dark,
> freedom and pain, joy and grief.
> Islands are born in volcanic action
> at once savage and beautiful.
> Vegetation is death and rebirth,
> light and darkness,
> frugality and abundance.
> Plants, animals and human beings
> are birthed from the dark
> through the pain and the death
> of the breaking of the seed into the light of life.
Jesus suffered and died on the cross,
while darkness struck the earth
in the middle of the day,
overcoming fear
and the old instinct of self-preservation,
into the birth of a new risen life,
leaving behind him the old.

Human life, like all life, is a paradox.
We are its *absolute* center,

and yet our existence is *relative.*
Human wholeness and attention
depend on bonds with mother, father,
earth and other;
yet, these links must be severed,
for only a degree of separateness leads to development
and personal responsibility.
    Young people tied to mother's apron strings
    cannot become themselves.
    If parent, friend or lover attempts to possess
    or direct the thought of the loved one,
    growth is stunted in both,
    as the loved one is gradually reduced to an "object."
    Genuine relationship demands giving
    and discreetly withholding:
    love, freedom, light, shadow,
    and a glimpse of endless horizons in equal balance
    are called for.
Health is a question of balance
of an innumerable number of cells,
microbes, bacteria and parasites,
keeping each other carefully checked,
allowing mutual development and growth,
granting each other the light of day,
but also keeping each other in darkness
and restraint to a great extent.
    Healing is always restoring the balanced integration
    of all the parts of an organism,
    redressing an imbalance
    that occurred
    because a part tried to devour the whole,
    and was not withheld in its fear
    for shadow and pain, compassion and love.

Throughout life there is a temptation
to cling to cherished people, places and times,
ideas and standpoints, to the me, mine and self.
But in order that novelty may become part of our personality
we have to withhold, to die to part of our "self."
For novelty to enter we must be empty of prejudice.
    Life is therefore a series

of small but painful deaths and rebirths.
Change is always painful:
a child must be weaned,
an adolescent must rebel against parental authority
to ensure his or her personal development.
Change is everywhere,
happening from moment to moment,
"in the smile,
in the tear,
under the dead leaf,
in vagrant thoughts
in the fullness of love."[1]
Pain is part of the cosmic process
it is the condition of growth.
The more we live the more pain we experience
when loyalties conflict and we appear to betray
religion, family, institution or country.
It is difficult to be faithful to all human values
at the same time.
When does compromise
become moral suicide?
Knowing about the fullness of life,
about cosmos, eros, and mythos,
emptiness and pain will hit us hard,
for grieving is proportionate to loss,
nothingness to everythingness.[2]
We grieve at the denial of life
in so much of the existing life system.
Sometimes from the very beginning,
but almost definitely from our first day at school,
our lives are directed
to *having* rather than to *being*
in a finite world
where the affluence of the minority
rises steadily in proportion
to the appalling increase of poverty of the majority,
whose royal personhood and cosmic share
are not even suspected.
We must surely ask ourselves the question
whether our "success"
or that of our family and friends

is not at the cost
of someone's else's failure or frustration.
Not only human beings are hit
by this unwillingness to be together.
The blue and green Earth jewel
is losing a species a day,
as moral aims are subjected to economic greed.
It might be that today
we are wiping out a plant with medicinal properties
to heal the breakdown in immune systems
which reflects the planetary catastrophe.
Leaves on the Tree of Life,
we are responsible
for the healing of the nations.

Knowing joy one experiences pain,
and knowing delight one feels sorrow.
Exuberance, births, compassion:
if you appreciate the dazzling wonder of creation,
can you suffer the wanton destruction
of the dark and mysterious tropical rain forest?
Nurturing human dignity and autonomy,
can you allow valium, cocaine, or excessive alcohol
to obliterate the pregnant darkness of mind?
In England, for example, a violent crime is committed
every eight minutes
by those under the influence of excessive alcohol.
Tasting fullness of life
can you deny the pain and murder
of those to whom life is denied
because of hunger and drought,
political prowess, greed, or distress?
Knowing that for every pound of hamburger
8000 pounds of fossil water are lost in Kansas,
and for every bushel of grain
five bushels of topsoil in Iowa,
can you eat your meat and roll,
without weeping for the laying waste to the future?[3]
Accepting all of yourself
will you suppress the darkness of anger,
such as spurred Jesus
to chase the money makers

from the Temple?
There is the need to accept our shadows,
there is a need to accept our pain,
it is in that darkness that the need to change lurks,
it is in that shade that conversion is possible.
> From childbirth to death
> we are usually swept into oblivion
> at the approach of pain
> which, in a society obsessed
> with success and macho image,
> is seen as a sign of weakness.
Within the spiritual tradition in a religious community
closely linked to the establishment,
pain was seen as the possibility of glorifying in self,
boosting your ego,
dominating suffering with sheer will power,
not accepting it really, and consequently not seeing it
as a reason for conversion, as a seed for new growth,
not willing to let go, not willing to enter the dark
neither in ourselves, nor in the others.
> The high and increased teenage suicide rate,
> the desperate urge for stimulants and depressants
> testify to our inability to share pain,
> though we are probably
> moved by the shudder of a falling tree
> and by the groan of an animal in pain.
> Entering into another's pain would bring
> change, growth, and liberation.
> Carers of AIDS patients often feel privileged,
> they confess, for that very reason.
> *Salvation is nothing but*
> *organic solidarity.*
> Privatized and uncommunicated pain and suffering
> are crippling and hide our place in the whole.
If we leave our concerns,
even our images of perpetual growth and success,
and have the courage to be the real ones,
we and the others are,
we would transform ourselves.
> We would experience, as lovers do,
> nothingness and everythingness,

as all barriers of anima and animus,
joy and pain, religion and nation,
tribe and family dissolve in a peak moment
undreamed of.
With *merrier senses*
and a *second dangerous innocence*
the status quo
would be sorely lacking.
Compassion and creativity,
birthed in the darkness and mystery of shared pain,
would create a new world where nothing is withheld.
That this is not just wishful thinking,
or a beautiful dream,
is proved each time
an extraordinary disaster strikes.
When southern England
was hit by a hurricane,
as they had never experienced before,
people were not only seen
grieving for thousands of fallen trees,
speaking of them as children,
but amidst scenes of devastation,
usually only seen on television
in far off parts of the world,
people spoke to and helped each other
who normally would never do so.
Barriers of prejudice and strangeness
slipped away with the power lines
in a greater urgency.
Weather is no respecter of persons
and when pain is shared, life is richer
as compassion *(and our wholeness)* wells up.
It appears that we must wait
for extraordinary natural disasters
to release the same power as Jesus did
when he enabled five thousand
to share their bread and their fish.

The last and ultimate shadow
we carry in us is death,
all day and all night,

the darkest, inescapable shadow of all.
Mircea Eliade
suggested that the initiation rites
we mentioned before give death a positive function
and, knowing how to die,
one can truly live.[4]
This belief seems to recur in all major religions.
Initiation embodies death and rebirth
the passover from old to new,
from immature to adult throughout life.
    "All of the life of the earth dies,
    all of the time,
    in the same volume as the new life
    that dazzles us each morning,
    each spring."[5]
At death the family will share the joyful passage
to join the ancestors, finally becoming one of them.[6]
    This is why an old African like Jomo Kenyatta,
    the first President of Kenya,
    called his whole large family to him
    some days before his death.
Yet we have lost Sister Death of Saint Francis,
the "helper" and "elegant easy-paced conveyance"
of contemporary Ustad Khalilullah Khalili.[7]
Death is whispered about, not prepared for,
it has become a human, sterile event.
Not understanding death
Western society misses the infinite preciousness of life.
    If we could embrace
    the necessity and mystery of death
    we would live fuller lives.
    Paradoxically, insecurity and fear of death
    lead individuals and governments
    to invent ever deadlier weapons
    which threaten us with darkness beyond darkness:
    total extinction.
We hasten that which we fear in a vicious circle.
Otto Rank, psychologist,
suggests that fear of death
is as characteristic of a patriarchal society
as is fear of the earth, of women

and fear of animals.[8]
    Eros and the love of life are driven away
    with our innermost dark dragons.
It is with death as with our other shadows.
Death is all we are not,
it is our negation,
death is the dark in which our light does not shine,
it is the land we did not travel,
the existence we never were,
the time we did not pass,
the space we never occupied,
the lives we never lived.
Death is the limitation, the cutting edge
between what we are and what we are not,
but once will be.
    Death is the loudest invitation,
    the clearest admonition
    to discreetly withhold
    the celebration of the lives we lead,
    the light we enjoy, the music we hear,
    the perfumes we smell, the food we eat,
    the water and wine we drink,
    the lover we embrace.
All that, is not all there is;
there is so much more awaiting us.
    It is only by dancing with that shadow,
    our last and final partner here on earth,
    sister or brother death,
    that we—swirling and swirling around—
    will overcome every abyss,
    filling all the valleys, straightening all the paths.
    Embracing her or him, we will find our place,
    alight, and live,
    finally interconnected with all,
    without any shadow being cast any more,
    as they are now all accepted,
    light filling them all,
    heaven galore,
    the summit of life,
    alleluia!

CHAPTER TEN

THE TREE OF LIFE

Earth, shall I return, shall I return to the tree?
This is the tree that grew from sleep to Eden,
Bore blossoms, and babe, and a million, million summers,
Its leaves have whispered passions: language to lovers.

And every spring has hung
The incarnate God bleeding away among its branches
Whose dying is perennial as the vine.

Kathleen Raine

I am the vine and you are the branches.

Jesus

You are the forest
You are all the great trees
    in the forest

You are bird and beast
    playing in and out
    of all the trees
O Lord white as jasmine.

Mahadeviyakka

Our final withholding
is the end of a cycle.
The leaf falls,
in the fullness of her color
it falls and withers away,
but the tree lives on
from the gift of the leaves we were.
We remain, now in another way,
taken up in the whole.
We were not cut off to be thrown in the fire,
—as Jesus said of those who did not contribute—
but live on for ever and ever,
and even our mortal frame is taken up again
by those who follow us
as the earth around the tree
with all its molds and fungi
is another source and wellspring of its new life.
 Thrusting upwards
 with an energy of her own
 a tree showers her energy
 in bud, leaf, flower, fruit and seed,
 sending down powerful roots
 and—notwithstanding gravity—
 growing up higher and higher.
 Children play in her, climbing her branches,
 lovers find solitude and intimacy in her shade,
 workers rest under her during the day.
 Sitting around the fire
 of her fallen branches
 in the warmth, light, and fragrance,
 grandparents tell their stories
 during the evening,
 while children crouch nearby
 to listen as long as they can,
 while bird, insect, and animal snuggle high
 in their shelters and nests.
A tree
spangled with myriad leaves,
with space to be herself,
holds together death and life,
dark and light,

earth and heaven,
vegetable, mineral, and animal.
No wonder that the tree always has been seen
as a symbol of God and life.
Farmhouses and homes all over Europe and America
had that tree traditionally
in their front door window decorations.
Africa is full of carvings of this tree of life
in the hardest woods it produces,
teeming with animals and birds,
fruits, plants, flowers, children, and ancestors.
So many of us have been trying
to trace our family trees as far back as possible.
The further we go, the better we feel;
the deeper our roots, the nobler we are.
Can we doubt our royal personhood
considering the depth of our common human roots?
Trees,
the largest and oldest living things in this world,
symbolize earth's
"groping toward the steep heaven
whom she childs us by."[1]
We come from the trees,
millions of years our ancestry lived in them.
Maybe our dreams of flying
and the sudden sense of falling
are nostalgic reminiscences of days gone by.
We miss those graceful leaps and ecstatic moments
of weightlessness in the high canopy.[2]
Does not every child
spontaneously climb the trees it sees,
building a shelter in it, if it can?
Our coccyx seems to be the only silent trace
and discrete reminder of our tail.
For thousands of years people have sheltered
in tropical rain forests
which have developed
for nine hundred million years.
Trees are protection, trees are life.
They are the lungs of the world,
the producers of the oxygen all life needs,

they gentle the climate, check the desert,
attract the rain, keep the earth together,
and maintain the soil's ecological balance.
    One in four chemicals found
    in the drugstores in a shopping mall
    contain compounds from rain forest species.
    Seventy percent of plants
    with anti-cancerous properties come from them.
    Almost everything we eat for breakfast
    originated there
    and Amazonia holds one in five
    of all the birds on earth.[3]
    Threats to the trees
    are threats to the Tree of Life;
    what befalls them, befalls us.

One day, in the Himalayas,
a small girl was collecting firewood
when she saw men with axes and saws
creeping into the forest.
She ran and told her story to the wise woman of the village,
who recognized the paper company men.
As there were no men in the village
at this time of the day
twenty-one women and seven children ran
and physically clung to the trees
despite the threats from the armed men.
They kept embracing the trees in a hug
called *chipko*,
remembering how two centuries earlier
thirty-five women had been killed in a similar attempt
to protect their forest and life.
They succeeded as a government inquiry concluded
that cutting the trees would mean
the end of their livelihood,
their fires, their homes, their fields and their lives.[4]
    Even now,
    at this very moment,
    you are contacting
    these thoughts and your own inner response
    on paper made from trees.

In our ever-growing communication
tree pulp plays an essential role,
notwithstanding our electronic progress.
It is through trees that we communicate
our thoughts, passions, dreams, love and hatred.
It is from forests in the world
that the printed word comes to us,
it is from vernal wood
that our impulses meet each other,
that ideas grow,
knowledge increases,
and dreams and visions are communicated.

O never harm the dreaming world
the world of green, the world of leaves,
but let its million palms unfold,
the adoration of the trees.[5]

Jesus again and again
is related and relates
to this image of the tree.
He stems from the root of Jesse,[6]
depicted in branching candlesticks in synagogues
and stained glass windows in cathedrals.
He was a woodworker, a carpenter,
who dying on a tree opened his arms
to embrace in a gesture,
as wide open as that of the branches on a tree
the whole of cosmic reality.
Before that Jesus had a vision,
he saw that we all belong together
as the leaves, branches, fruits, and seeds on a tree.
He said that belonging together like this,
we should love the other
as we love ourselves.
This interdependence is no longer
only a mystical vision,
the dream of a visionary like Isaiah
who already "saw" all peoples coming together.
It is no longer only
the product of a fertile religious imagination.

It is a concrete reality.

In October 1987 stock markets in the world
fell like a row of dominoes:
Wall Street, Tokyo, London, Hong Kong.
The effect of that fall touched all of us,
from the poorest hovel in Africa
to the richest mansion in Japan.
This financial message that we all belong together
struck the world harder
than papal encyclicals and episcopal pastoral letters
struck their congregations.
Since the Second World War this interdependence
has become clearer and clearer
from a political, economic, social,
but also from the "organic" and "medical" point of view.
We come forth out of the decisions of the past,
we are imagining the present and forming it,
and this definitely has an influence on the future.
> It is not only true of the human being,
> the rest of nature is involved, too.
> The stones we throw in the water,
> drawing their ripples in the pond in front of us
> have an influence all over the world.
> So has the song we compose, play, or even listen to;
> the depth we fathom in ourselves,
> the God we meet
> and the prayers we pray!
> The movement of a butterfly's wing
> might be the cause of the next hurricane!
John XXIII could speak of the moral structural defect
that makes it impossible for us to realize
the international common good.
This structural defect
is also partly the reason
that we cannot "give in" to our pity,
that we are still unable to establish justice,
that we in fact cannot "live" together,
that we cannot face the reality of the world
in which we live.
Still very much growth has to be made.

Not able to realize the national common good,
and sometimes not even the family common good,
we definitely are still very far
from being able to realize
the international common good.
The interdependence we speak about,
has not yet brought about the moral change
we need to realize.
The ambiguity remains,
we still manufacture lethal weapons at enormous costs
to defend ourselves against all those
with whom we belong together.
We still kill their culture and custom
in conversion to a Western Christianity
which often ignores the good,
God within them.
Even the U.S. bishops seem to send different signals
in their last pastoral statements.
Though they, too, admit that we belong together,
they do not forbid the making of atomic weapons
in order to destroy others,
though those others would not be able to die,
without tearing humanity apart in incurable pieces.

    The tree image is a paradox,
    it is a symbol of a whole,
    it is a symbol of a part.
    We are the vine,
    we are the branches.
    Each leaf on the tree
    embodies its life and its growth,
    and its groping for time and space;
    just as each of us embodies
    the wonder of human existence.
As individuals we can't do very much;
a leaf alone is bound to die,
and so would a branch if on its own.
We are in all this together,
grace is all together,
grace is life, there is nothing else,
we belong together,
one is the nose, loving incense,

the other the eye, loving color,
the ear listening to oratory and music,
the hand working effectively,
the feet that love dancing.
Blue should be blue and not red,
for if all colors were like all other colors
everything would be grey.
A trumpet should sound like a trumpet,
salt should not taste like pepper,
nor nutmeg taste like cinnamon.
It is the harmony of sounds and tastes
that make life so rich.
Cinnamon alone is not edible
lard alone is hopeless.
A clarinet at full blast is nice
but is better in harmony
with other instruments.
Even humanity on its own
would be without the sounds of birds and beasts,
the rustling of the eucalyptus tree,
the splash of fresh fish in blue water,
the silhouette of a palm in a hot tropical night
and the stuff and will to live on.

> Sleep at the tree's root, where the night is spun
> Into the stuff of worlds, listen to the winds,
> The tides and the night's harmonies and know
> All that you knew before you began to forget
> Before you became estranged from your own being.[7]

The generations belong together, too.
The young child intuitively knows
to be bound up
with ocean and tree,
water and life,
rebirth and death.
Growing up
we become aware of our apparent separateness.
The adolescent feels and thinks
the whole world hers or his.
        As an adult we learn

that we cannot exist without everything else.
Becoming older
we ponder the miracle of human existence
of what it means to be the growing tip
of earth's youngest species.
If we blossom
in relationship, art, play,
and mystical experience,
our wisdom will be greater.
Taking time to sit under the Tree by the Spring,
free of the worries of the younger,
we will be that spring for others.
We will plunge the depth of the all,
letting the demands of universal becoming
flow through us.
We will touch anew the universal consciousness
of child, mystic, poet, and artist
as we embrace the perennial suffering of the world
so that the Word may endlessly give birth.
    It is so essential,
    so important,
    so absolutely crucial,
    that we take care
    that generations in family and community
    remain telling their stories
    and reflecting together!

Awareness is growing, it is growing everywhere.
Schools are reorganized in view of our global future:
Kestrel Manor in Nairobi,
Rudolph Steiner Schools in Europe,
scores of alternative schools in the USA,
A former Assistant Secretary General of the United Nations,
Robert Mueller advocates a world core curriculum
organized around four basic harmonies:
    our planetary home and place in the universe,
    the human family,
    our place in time,
    and the miracle of human existence.
Political leaders are coming together,
international business is under scrutiny,

even the world's debt brings peoples around tables,
they would otherwise never sit around.
Hundreds of Networks and Telephone Trees
are taking up more and more issues.
Theologians start listening to the stories of the oppressed,
Church leaders speak of "inter-dependence,"
praying together for justice and peace,
embracing the *passion of political love*
and allowing themselves to delight anew in God.[8]

    We live in Presence
    diffused throughout the Universe.
    The Tree of Life is the Incarnation
    which inspires tenderly poignant feelings
    towards mineral, vegetable, animal, and human
    manifestations of the Divine.

In this New Age we are penetrating
mists of nationalism and selfishness,
that have been too long hanging around,
blocking our vision and hindering our growth,
to reach greater affinity with the demands of the All.
We contemplate anew the heavens,
the ozone layer and acid rain,
our water supplies and mineral reserves,
the lilies of the field,
the whales and our human neighbors.

    It is our privilege
    to grow in exuberant unity
    in the arms of Mother Earth,
    appreciating the gift of existence
    believing as people did from the very beginning,
    that the gift should always move,
    as the sun, moon, stars, wind, and ocean always do.
    Life may be found or lost, but never possessed.
    The past and the future are not ours
    but the living moment is,
    our role has to be played now.
    We are not the oil, but the point of combustion;
    not the air, but the flashpoint where light is born.
    We know life to the degree that we are transparent,
    and willing to let it flow through us,
    passing on our gift of creativity.

Aware
of our threads of matter and dream
drawn from the primordial matrix;
of the fountain of life thrusting ever upwards
from deep within us;
of our glistening place in the cosmic web,
of our individuality and universality
 —particle and wave—
of being a "per-son"
through whom all creation voices herself;
we awaken to the original goodness of creation.
Though sometimes consisting only
of early childhood memories,
scraps of stories and myths,
tattered remnants of old connections and bonds,
each of us must return
to the serene completeness
of our beginning,
before we began to forget.
    Radical amazement will stir again our creativity:
    the Tree of Life,
    divine cradle and crucible,
    is rediscovered
    and her mystery revealed.

Over every living thing which is to spring up, to grow, to flower, to ripen during this day, say again the words: This is my Body. And over every death force which waits in readiness to corrode, to wither, to cut down, speak again your commanding words which express the supreme mystery of life: This is my Blood.[9]

NOTES

INTRODUCTION

1. Michael Ignatieff, "Paradigm Lost," *Times Literary Supplement*, No. 4405, September 4-11, 1987, p. 944.

CHAPTER 2

1. William Blake, "Auguries of Innocence," in *Blake: Poems and Letters Selected by Jacob Bronowski*, London, Penguin Books, 1986.

2. Elizabeth Anne Byrne, *An Analysis of Kestrel Manor School with Reference to the Anisa Model*, Antioch University, 1987, pp. 24-25.

3. Julius Nyerere, former President of the East African country Tanzania, observed: "[Africa] can draw from its traditional heritage the recognition of 'society' as an extension of the basic family unit. But it can no longer confine the idea of the social family within the limits of the tribe, nor indeed, of the nation."

4. "One of the manifest destinies of Africa, therefore, is to promote the universalization of the creative harmony model of living throughout the world. The West has plagued the world long enough with its conflict model of thinking and acting. While the West sees society as made up of incompatible individual interests, which are in a state of perpetual conflict and bargaining for the maximization of success/victory, the indigenous African sees society as founded on creative harmony and unity in duality." N.K. Dzobo, "Black Civilization as Cultural Product of Conceptual Creativity," Paper presented at FESTAC, 1977, *Cross Currents*, xxviii, 4, 1978, p. 464.

CHAPTER 3

1. Dag Hammarskjöld, *Markings*, transl. W.H. Auden and Leif Sjoberg, Faber and Faber, London, 1980, p. 89.

CHAPTER 4

1. Jonathan Cape, London, 1983. "There are many who say that for the

primitive, life was and is, in Hobbessian terms, nasty, brutish and short. On the whole, anthropologists have found otherwise, and over the years have accumulated an enormous amount of data to support their view. If we measure a culture's worth by the longevity of its population, the sophistication of its technology, the material comforts it offers, then, many primitive cultures have little to offer to us, that is true. But our study of the life cycle will show that in terms of a conscious dedication to human relationships that are both affective and effective, the primitive is ahead of us all the way. He is working at it at every stage of life, from infancy to death, while playing just as much as while praying, whether at work or at home his life is governed by his conscious quest for social order. Each individual learns the social consciousness as he grows up, and the lesson is constantly reinforced until the day he dies; and because of that social consciousness each individual is a person of worth and value and important to society also from the day of birth to the day of death." p. 21.

CHAPTER 5

1. Kathleen Raine in "Lyric," *Collected Poems*, Hamish, London, 1956.

2. Fritjof Capra, *The Schumacher Lectures*, ed. Satish Kumar, Penguin, London, 1982, p. 142.

3. See Rainer Maria Rilke, *Letters to a Young Poet*, translated and with a foreword by Stephen Mitchell, Random House, New York, 1984, pp. 37-38.

4. Quoted in Matthew Fox, *Original Blessing: A Primer in Creation Spirituality*, Bear and Co., New Mexico, 1983, p. 283.

CHAPTER 6

1. Pierre Boncenne, Jean Guitton, *Lire*, No. 121, October 1985, p. 136.

2. "Although this unity of the entire world order was perceived by primitive *(sic!)* peoples, affirmed by great civilizations, explained in creation myths the world over, outlined by Plato in his *Timaeus* and given extensive presentation by Newton in his *Principia*, nowhere was the full genetic relatedness of the universe presented with such clarity as by the scientists of the 20th century. To Isaac Newton we are especially indebted for our understanding of the gravitational attraction of every physical reality to every other physical reality in the universe, an attraction that finds its ultimate fulfillment in the affective attraction that exists throughout the human community. To Darwin we are indebted for our understanding of the genetic unity of the entire web of living beings. To Einstein and his theories of relativity we are indebted for an awareness of how to think the dynamics of relatedness in the uni-

verse.....Everything is intimately present to everything else in the universe. Nothing is completely itself without everything else." Thomas Berry, "The American College in the Ecological Age," pp.3-4, quoted in Patricia M. Mische, *Star Wars and the State of Our Souls*, Winston Press, Minneapolis, 1985, p.125.

3. D.H. Lawrence, *Apocalypse*, Granada, London, 1981, p.50.

4. John 1: 1.

5. Paolo Freire, *Pedagogy of the Oppressed*, transl. Myra Ramos, Penguin, London, 1975, p. 60.

6. London ITV," State of the Nation," January 19, 1987.

7. E.F. Schumacher, *Small Is Beautiful: A Study of Economics As If People Mattered*, Abacus, London, 1976, p. 34.

8. Pierre Teilhard de Chardin, *On Love and Happiness*, Harper & Row, San Francisco, 1984, pp.45-46.

9. Cf. Ephesians 4: 13.

10. Pierre Teilhard de Chardin, ibid. pp. 44-45.

11. Colossians 2: 2.

CHAPTER 7

1. Okot p' Bitek, "The Woman with Whom I Share My Husband," in *Song of Lawino*, East African Publishing House, Nairobi, 1966, p. 60.

2. Lois Ellfeldt, *Dance From Magic to Art*, W.C. Brown Co, Dubuque, Iowa, 1976, p. 16-18.

3. "Every man who has once touched the level of the impersonal is changed with a responsibility towards all human beings: to safeguard not their persons, but whatsoever frail potentialities are hidden within them from passing over to the impersonal." *The Simone Weil Reader*, ed. George E. Panichas, David McKay Co.. New York, 1977, p. 320.

4. Susanne Langer, *Feeling and Form: A Theory of Art* developed from "Philosophy in a New Key," Routledge and Kegan Paul Ltd., 1976, p. 40.

5. See Matthew Fox, *Original Blessing*, p. 176.

6. "Facts about the Arts," *New Internationalist*, Feb. 1985.

7. Lois Ellfeldt, *op. cit.* p. 6.

8. Plato, *The Republic*, transl. Desmond Lee, Penguin, London, 1974, p. 163.

9. *Ibid.* p. 85.

CHAPTER 8

1. Adrienne Rich, *Of Woman Born: Motherhood as Experience and Institution*, W. W. Norton and Co., New York, 1976, p. 3.

2. Abraham Maslow, quoted in Frank Goble, *The Third Force: The Psychology of Abraham Maslow*, Grossman, New York, 1970, p. 49.

3. There is an other way in which we can look at this "complementarity": "...in the mid-1970s, Ken Wilber, a consciousness researcher, developed a theory he calls "the spectrum of consciousness,' which describes various levels of consciousness as parts of one continuum he calls "mind." Wilber has insisted that over the history of humankind these levels of consciousness have become fragmented and increasingly treated as if they were separate. He describes different Western therapies and Eastern religions as addressing different bands of this spectrum of consciousness, each speaking to what Bohm would call a relatively autonomous subtotality. He envisions ultimate freedom as the recognition that all the bands of the spectrum are really one whole movement of mind which extends beyond the individual into the universe at large." John P. Briggs and F. David Peat, *Looking Glass Universe: The Emerging Science of Wholeness*, Cornerstone Library, Simon & Schuster, New York, 1984, p. 279.

4. Frank C. Goble, *The Third Force: The Psychology of Abraham Maslow*, Grossman, New York, 1970, p. 52.

5. Quoted in Joseph Campbell, *The Inner Reaches of Outer Space*, Alfred van der Marck, New York, 1986, p. 112.

6. The Gospel of Thomas, 45: 30-33.

7. E.A. Byrne, *op. cit.*, p. 4.

8. Briggs and Peat, *op. cit.*, p. 276.

9. See *Motivational Personality*, Harper & Row, New York, 1970.

10. Lewis Thomas, *The Medusa and the Snail: More Notes of a Biology Watcher*, Bantam, New York, 1980, p. 128.

CHAPTER 9

1. J. Krishnamurti, *The First and the Last Freedom*, Victor Gollancz Ltd., 1969, p. 287.

2. Matthew Fox, *Original Blessing*, p.130.

3. Lewis Hide, *op. cit.*

4. Quoted in Pierre Erny, *The Child and His Environment in Black Africa: An Essay on Black Education*, Transl. G. Wanjohi, Oxford University

Press, Nairobi, 1981, p. 148.

5. Lewis Thomas, *The Lives of a Cell: Notes of a Biology Watcher*, Bantam, New York, 1983, p.115.

6. "Remaining in West Africa... it is important to note that the whole point of going on the last journey is to become one of the ancestors. Now, the significance of the ancestors consists simply in this, that they watch over the affairs of the living members of their families, helping deserving ones, and punishing the delinquent....Ancestors are there to see to the good of the living. There is, of course, a reciprocal side to this. Reciprocity is a strong feature of African society; it is in fact, a feature of any moral community. Accordingly the living feel not only beholden to the ancestors for their help and protection, but also positively obliged to do honor to them and render service to them as appropriate." Kwasi Wiredu, *Death and the Afterlife in African Culture*, paper read at the Wilson Institute, Washington D.C., 27 October 1987, pp. 2-3.

7. Idries Shah, *Learning How to Learn: Psychology and Spirituality in the Sufi Way*, Penguin, London, 1983, p. 265.

8. Matthew Fox, *op. cit.* p. 135.

CHAPTER 10

1. Gerard Manley Hopkins, "Ash-Boughs," in *Poems and Prose*, Penguin, London, 1973, stanza a, lines 10-11.

2. Carl Sagan, *The Dragons of Eden: Speculations on the Evolution of Human Intelligence*, Hodder and Stoughton, London, 1977, p. 83.

3. Friends of the Earth, *Rainforests*, London, 1985.

4. *For Every Child a Tree*, UNEP, Nairobi, 1982, p. 25.

5. Chief Seattle, quoted in *The Gaia Atlas of Planet Management*, ed. Norman Myers, Pan Books, London, 1985, p. 159.

6. Isaiah 11:1.

7. Kathleen Raine, "Message from Home," in *The Collected Poems*, Hamish Hamilton, London, 1968, stanza 5, 2-6.

8. Thomas Cullinan, *The Passion of Political Love*, Sheed and Ward, London, 1987.

9. Pierre Teilhard de Chardin, *Hymn of the Universe*, Collins, Fontana, London, 1976, p. 23.